D0695787

BEHAVIORAL ANALYSIS OF VIOLENT CRIME: SELECTED READINGS

JOHN ROBERT CENCICH, J.S.D.

THE HAGUE PRESS INTERNATIONAL

Copyright © by John Robert Cencich
All rights reserved

Library of Congress Cataloging-in-Publication Data
Cencich, John R., 1957 –
    Behavioral Analysis of Violent Crime: Selected
    readings /John R. Cencich (ed.)
    Pages cm (studies in crime and public policy)
    ISBN 978-0-9913293-3-5   (paperback)
    1. Federal Bureau of Investigation *Law Enforcement
        Bulletin.*
    2. National Institute of Justice. 3. Supreme Court
    Cases.

Printed in the United States
The Hague Press International
First Edition

Contents

Introduction to Behavioral Analysis of Violent Crime

By

John Robert Cencich, J.S.D.

THE JOURNEY INTO THE CRIMINAL MIND IS A fascinating one indeed. Many of you have seen the movie *Silence of the Lambs* with FBI special agent trainee Clarice Starling hot on the trail of "Buffalo Bill," a serial killer who eviscerates the bodies of his victims. And in order to do so successfully, she consults with Dr. Hannibal Lecter, an imprisoned serial killer who is known for eating his victims and a psychiatrist in his own right.

While it certainly goes without saying that the real world is not always reflected accurately in film and literature, what lies in the abyss of the human mind can shock the conscious of humanity and far exceed the imaginations of Hollywood. This is something I know firsthand. Not only have I seen the death and carnage of man's inhumanity to man, but I have personally tracked down and interviewed humans— some of the world's worst criminals—who have raped, tortured, murdered, and exterminated fellow members of the human race.

This textbook is intended to serve as a reader for undergraduate and graduate coursework involving the theory behind the criminal mind and the behavioral analysis of violent crime. Accordingly, you will be studying—from a theoretical perspective—topics that include the origins of criminal behavior, human aggression and violence, criminal psychopathy, and mental disorders. Through the textbook, you will be provided an opportunity to apply some of the theoretical underpinnings to real world situations.

I have specially chosen the readings, which range from U.S. Supreme Court Cases and statutory instruments to the full text of Fyodor Dostoyevsky's (my favorite author of all time) short story, *The Dream of a Ridiculous Man*. I have even included relevant excerpts of my book, *The Devil's Garden: A War Crimes Investigator's Story*. You will also find discussion questions and critical thinking exercises that often draw upon my own professional experiences investigating and analyzing violent crime.

I am confident that if you put your time and effort into this course, you will find it a rewarding one albeit a shocking—and sometimes disturbing—journey into the minds of killers, rapists, and sadists.

JOHN ROBERT CENCICH
DOCTOR OF JURIDICAL SCIENCE AND
PROFESSOR OF CRIMINAL JUSTICE

INSANITY

By

John Robert Cencich, J.S.D.

THE BEHAVIORAL ANALYSIS OF VIOLENT CRIME QUITE necessarily revolves around the offender's state of mind. Frequently the analysis relates to the mental state at the time of the alleged criminal act, but it can also include the accused's mental capacity to defend himself or assist n his defense during key legal steps such as the trial.

Contrary to popular belief, very few defendants in criminal cases plead the affirmative defense of insanity, and even fewer actually succeed. Nevertheless, the notion of insanity, is a legal one, can quite literally mean life or death for defendant, depending upon the jurisdiction within which he is tried.

In very basic terms, the legal test for insanity rests on whether the defendant knew what he was doing at the time of the act. In the British case of *R v. Arnold* (1724), the Court formulated this as, "whether the accused is totally deprived of his understanding and memory and knew what he was doing "no more than a wild beast or a brute, or an infant".

In modern times, courts will often rely on the opinions of mental health professionals in making such determinations. To help you better understand these concepts, I have provided the full text of the 1843 House of Lords speech in the *case of Daniel M'Naghten.*

DANIEL M'NAGHTEN'S CASE
House of Lords
Mews' Dig. i. 349; iv. 1112. S.C. 8 Scott N.R. 595; 1 C. and K. 130; 4 St. Tr. N.S. 847
May 26, June 19, 1843

The prisoner had been indicted for that he, on the 20th day of January 1843, at the parish of Saint Martin in the Fields, in the county of Middlesex, and within the jurisdiction of the Central Criminal Court, in and upon one Edward Drummond, feloniously, wilfully, and of his malice aforethought, did make an assault; and that the said Daniel M'Naghten, a certain pistol of the value of 20's., loaded and charged with gunpowder and a leaden bullet (which pistol he in his right hand had and held), to, against and upon the said Edward Drummond, feloniously, wilfully, and of his malice aforethought, did shoot and discharge; and that the said Daniel M'Naghten, with the leaden bullet aforesaid, out of the pistol aforesaid, by force of the gunpowder, etc., the said Edward Drummond, in and upon the back of him the said Edward Drummond, feloniously, etc. did strike, penetrate and wound, giving to the said Edward Drummond, in and upon the back of the said Edward Drummond, one mortal wound, etc., of which mortal wound the said E. Drummond languished until the 25th of April and then died; and that by the means aforesaid, he the prisoner did kill and murder the said Edward Drummond. The prisoner pleaded Not guilty.

Evidence having been given of the fact of the shooting of Mr. Drummond, and of his death in consequence thereof, witnesses were called on the part of the prisoner, to prove that he was not, at the time of committing the act, in a sound state of mind.

The medical evidence was in substance this: That persons of otherwise sound mind, might be affected by morbid delusions: that the prisoner was in that condition: that a person so labouring under a morbid delusion, might have a moral perception of right and wrong, but that in the case of the prisoner it was a delusion which carried him away beyond the power of his own control, and left him no such perception; and that he was not capable of exercising any control over acts which had connection with his delusion: that it was of the nature of the disease with which the prisoner was affected, to go on gradually until it had reached a climax, when it burst forth with irresistible intensity: that a man might go on for years quietly, though at the same time under its influence, but would all at once break out into the most extravagant and violent paroxysms.

Some of the witnesses who gave this evidence, had previously examined the prisoner: others had never seen him till he appeared in Court, and they formed their opinions on hearing the evidence given by the other witnesses.

Lord Chief Justice Tindal (in his charge):--The question to be determined is, whether at the time the act in question was committed, the prisoner had or had not the use of his understanding, so as to know that he was doing a wrong or wicked act. If the jurors should be of opinion that the prisoner was not sensible, at the time he committed it, that he was violating the laws both of God and man, then he would be entitled to a verdict in his favour: but if, on the contrary, they were of opinion that when he committed the act he was in a sound state of mind, then their verdict must be against him. Verdict, Not guilty, on the ground of insanity.

This verdict, and the question of the nature and extent of the unsoundness of mind which would excuse the commission of a felony of this sort, having been made the subject of debate in the House of Lords (the 6th and 13th March 1843; see Hansard's Debates, vol. 67, pp. 288, 714), it was determined to take the opinion of the Judges on the law governing such cases. Accordingly, on the 26th of May, all the Judges attended their Lordships, but no questions were then put.

On the 19th of June, the Judges again attended the House of Lords; when (no argument having been had) the following questions of law were propounded to them:

1st. What is the law respecting alleged crimes committed by persons afflicted with insane delusion, in respect of one or more particular subjects or persons: as, for instance, where at the time of the commission of the alleged crime, the accused knew he was acting contrary to law, but did the act complained of with a view, under the influence of insane delusion, of redressing or revenging some supposed grievance or injury, or of producing some supposed public benefit?

2d. What are the proper questions to be submitted to the jury, when a person alleged to be afflicted with insane delusion respecting one or more particular subjects or persons, is charged with the commission of a crime (murder, for example), and insanity is set up as a defence?

3d. In what terms ought the question to be left to the jury, as to the prisoner's state of mind at the time when the act was committed?

4th. If a person under an insane delusion as to existing facts, commits an offence in consequence thereof, is he thereby excused?

5th. Can a medical man conversant with the disease of insanity, who never saw the prisoner previously to the trial, but who was present during the whole trial and the examination of all the witnesses, be asked his opinion as to the state of the prisoner's mind at the time of the commission of the alleged crime, or his opinion whether the prisoner was conscious at the time of doing the act, that he was acting contrary to law, or whether he was labouring under any and what delusion at the time?

Mr. Justice Maule:--I feel great difficulty in answering the questions put by your Lordships on this occasion:--First, because they do not appear to arise out of and are not put with reference to a particular case, or for a particular purpose, which might explain or limit the generality of their terms, so that full answers to them ought to be applicable to every possible state of facts, not inconsistent with those assumed in the questions: this difficulty is the greater, from the practical experience both of the bar and the Court being confined to questions arising out of the facts of particular cases:--Secondly, because I have heard no argument at your Lordships' bar or elsewhere, on the subject of these questions; the want of which I feel the more, the greater are the number and extent of questions which might be raised in argument:--and Thirdly, from a fear of which I cannot divest myself, that as these questions relate to matters of criminal law of great importance and frequent occurrence, the answers to them by the Judges may embarrass the administration of justice, when they are cited in criminal trials.

For these reasons I should have been glad if my learned brethren would have joined me in praying your Lordships to excuse us from answering these questions; but as I do not think they ought to induce me to ask that indulgence for myself individually, I shall proceed to give such answers as I can, after the very short time which I have had to consider the questions, and under the difficulties I have mentioned; fearing that my answers may be as little satisfactory to others as they are to myself.

The first question, as I understand it, is, in effect, What is the law respecting the alleged crime, when at the time of the commission of it, the accused knew he was acting contrary to the law, but did the act with a view, under the influence of insane delusion, of redressing or revenging some supposed grievance or injury, or of producing some supposed public benefit?

If I were to understand this question according to the strict meaning of its terms, it would require, in order to answer it, a solution of all questions of law which could arise on the circumstances stated in the question, either by explicitly stating and answering such questions, or by stating some principles or rules which would suffice for their solution. I am quite unable to do so, and, indeed, doubt whether it be possible to be done; and therefore request to be permitted to answer the question only so far as it comprehends the question, whether a person, circumstanced as stated in the question, is, for that reason only, to be found not guilty of a crime respecting which the question of his guilt has been duly raised in a criminal proceeding?

And I am of opinion that he is not. There is no law, that I am aware of, that makes persons in the state described in the question not responsible for their criminal acts. To render a person irresponsible for crime on account of unsoundness of mind, the unsoundness should, according to the law as it has long been understood and held, be such as rendered him incapable of knowing right from wrong. The terms used in the question cannot be said (with reference only to the usage of language) to be equivalent to a description of this kind and degree of unsoundness of mind. If the state described in the question be one which involves or is necessarily connected with such an unsoundness, this is not a matter of law but of physiology, and not of that obvious and familiar kind as to be inferred without proof.

Second, the questions necessarily to be submitted to the jury, are those questions of fact which are raised on the record. In a criminal trial, the question commonly is, whether the accused be guilty or not guilty: but, in order to assist the jury in coming to a right conclusion on this necessary and ultimate question, it is usual and proper to submit such subordinate or intermediate questions, as the course which the trial has taken may have made it convenient to direct their attention to. What those questions are, and the manner of submitting them, is a matter of discretion for the Judge: a discretion to be guided by a consideration of all the circumstances attending the inquiry. In performing this duty, it is sometimes necessary or convenient to inform the jury as to the law; and if, on a trial such as is suggested in the question, he should have occasion to state what kind and degree of insanity would amount to a defence, it should be stated conformably to what I have mentioned in my answer to the first question, as being, in my opinion, the law on this subject.

Third, there are no terms which the Judge is by law required to use. They should not be inconsistent with the law as above stated, but should be such as, in the discretion of the Judge, are proper to assist the jury in coming to a right conclusion as to the guilt of the accused.

Fourth, the answer which I have given to the first question, is applicable, to this. Fifth, whether a question can be asked, depends, not merely on the questions of fact raised on the record, but on the course of the cause at the time it is proposed to ask it; and the state of an inquiry as to the guilt of a person charged with a crime, and defended on the ground of insanity, may be such, that such a question as either of those suggested, is proper to be asked and answered, though the witness has never seen the person before the trial, and though he has merely been present and heard the witnesses: these circumstances, of his never having seen the person before, and of his having merely been present at the trial, not being necessarily sufficient, as it seems to me, to exclude the lawfulness of a question which is otherwise lawful; though I will not say that an inquiry might not be in such a state, as that these circumstances should have such an effect.

Supposing there is nothing else in the state of the trial to make the questions suggested proper to be asked and answered, except that the witness had been present and heard the evidence; it is to be considered whether that is enough to sustain the question. In principle it is open to this objection, that as the opinion of the witness is founded on those conclusions of fact which he forms from the evidence, and as it does not appear what those conclusions are, it may be that the evidence he gives is on such an assumption of facts, as makes it irrelevant to the inquiry.

But such questions have been very frequently asked, and the evidence to which they are directed has been given, and has never, that I am aware of, been successfully objected to.

Evidence, most clearly open to this objection, and on the admission of which the event of a most important trial probably turned, was received in the case of The Queen v. M'Naghten, tried at the Central Criminal Court in March last, before the Lord Chief Justice, Mr. Justice Williams, and Mr. Justice Coleridge, in which counsel of the highest eminence were engaged on both sides; and I think the course and practice of receiving such evidence, confirmed by the very high authority of these Judges, who not only received it, but left it, as I understand, to the jury, without any remark derogating from its weight, ought to be held to warrant its reception, notwithstanding the objection in principle to which it may be open. In cases even where the course of practice in criminal law has been unfavourable to parties accused, and entirely contrary to the most obvious principle of justice and humanity, as well as those of law, it has been held that such practice constituted the law, and could not be altered without the authority of Parliament.

Lord Chief Justice Tindal:--My Lords, Her Majesty's Judges (with the exception of Mr. Justice Maule, who has stated his opinion to your Lordships), in answering the questions proposed to them by your Lordships' House, think it right, in the first place, to state that they have forborne entering into any particular discussion upon these questions, from the extreme and almost insuperable difficulty of applying those answers to cases in which the facts are not brought judicially before them. The facts of each particular case must of necessity present themselves with endless variety, and with every shade of difference in each case; and as it is their duty to declare the law upon each particular case, on facts proved before them, and after hearing argument of counsel thereon, they deem it at once impracticable, and at the same time dangerous to the administration of justice, if it were practicable, to attempt to make minute applications of the principles involved in the answers given by them to your Lordships' questions.

They have therefore confined their answers to the statement of that which they hold to be the law upon the abstract questions proposed by your Lordships; and as they deem it unnecessary, in this peculiar case, to deliver their opinions seriatim, and as all concur in the same opinion, they desire me to express such their unanimous opinion to your Lordships.

The first question proposed by your Lordships is this: "What is the law respecting alleged crimes committed by persons afflicted with insane delusion in respect of one or more particular subjects or persons: as, for instance, where at the time of the commission of the alleged crime the accused knew he was acting contrary to law, but did the act complained of with a view, under the influence of insane delusion, of redressing or revenging some supposed grievance or injury, or of producing some supposed public benefit ?"

In answer to which question, assuming that your Lordships' inquiries are confined to those persons who labour under such partial delusions only, and are not in other respects insane, we are of opinion that, notwithstanding the party accused did the act complained of with a view under the influence of insane delusion, of redressing or revenging some supposed grievance or injury, or of producing some public benefit, he is nevertheless punishable according to the nature of the crime committed, if he knew at the time of committing such crime that he was acting contrary to law; by which expression we understand your Lordships to mean the law of the land.

Your Lordships are pleaded to inquire of us, secondly, What are the proper questions to be submitted to the jury, where a person alleged to be afflicted with insane delusion respecting one or more particular subjects or persons, is charged with the commission of a crime (murder, for example), and insanity is set up as a defence?" And, thirdly, "In what terms ought the question to be left to the jury as to the prisoner's state of mind at the time when the act was committed?"

And as these two questions appear to us to be more conveniently answered together, we have to submit our opinion to be, that the jurors ought to be told in all cases that every man is to be presumed to be sane, and to possess a sufficient degree of reason to be responsible for his crimes, until the contrary be proved to their satisfaction; and that to establish a defence on the ground of insanity, it must be clearly proved that, at the time of the committing of the act, the party accused as labouring under such a defect of reason, from disease of the mind, as not to know the nature and quality of the act he was doing; or, if he did know it, that he did not know he was doing what was wrong. The mode of putting the latter part of the question to the jury on these occasions has generally been, whether the accused at the time of doing the act knew the difference between right and wrong: which mode, though rarely, if ever, leading to any mistake with the jury, is not, as we conceive, so accurate when put generally and in the abstract, as when put with reference to the party's knowledge of right and wrong in respect to the very act with which he is charged. If the question were to be put as to the knowledge of the accused solely and exclusively with reference to the law of the land, it might tend to confound the jury, by inducing them to believe that an actual knowledge of the law of the land was essential in order to lead to a conviction; whereas the law is administered upon the principle that every one must be taken conclusively to know it, without proof that he does know it.

If the accused was conscious that the act was one which he ought not to do, and if that act was at the same time contrary to the law of the land, he is punishable; and the usual course therefore has been to leave the question to the jury, whether the party accused had a sufficient degree of reason to know that he was doing an act that was wrong: and this course we think is correct, accompanied with such observations and explanations as the circumstances of each particular case may require.

The fourth question which your Lordships have proposed to us is this:--"If a person under an insane delusion as to existing facts, commits an offence in consequence thereof, is he thereby excused?" To which question the answer must of course depend on the nature of the delusion: but, making the same assumption as we did before, namely, that he labours under such partial delusion only, and is not in other respects insane, we think he must be considered in the same situation as to responsibility as if the facts with respect to which the delusion exists were real. For example, if under the influence of his delusion he supposes another man to be in the act of attempting to take away his life, and he kills that man, as he supposes, in self-defence, he would be exempt from punishment. If his delusion was that the deceased had inflicted a serious injury to his character and fortune, and he killed him in revenge for such supposed injury, he would be liable to punishment.

The question lastly proposed by your Lordships is:-- "Can a medical man conversant with the disease of insanity, who never saw the prisoner previously to the trial, but who was present during the whole trial and the examination of all the witnesses, be asked his opinion as to the state of the prisoner's mind at the time of the commission of the alleged crime, or his opinion whether the prisoner was conscious at the time of doing the act that he was acting contrary to law, or whether he was labouring under any and what delusion at the time?"

In answer thereto, we state to your Lordships, that we think the medical man, under the circumstances supposed, cannot in strictness be asked his opinion in the terms above stated, because each of those questions involves the determination of the truth of the facts deposed to, which it is for the jury to decide, and the questions are not mere questions upon a matter of science, in which case such evidence is admissible. But where the facts are admitted or not disputed, and the question becomes substantially one of science only, it may be convenient to allow the question to be put in that general form, though the same cannot be insisted on as a matter of right.

Lord Brougham:--My Lords, the opinions of the learned Judges, and the very able manner in which they have been presented to the House, deserve our best thanks. One of the learned Judges has expressed his regret that these questions were not argued by counsel. Generally speaking, it is most important that in questions put for the consideration of the Judges, they should have all that assistance which is afforded to them by an argument by counsel: but at the same time, there can be no doubt of your Lordships' right to put, in this way, abstract questions of law to the Judges, the answer to which might be necessary to your Lordships in your legislative capacity. There is a precedent for this course, in the memorable instance of Mr. Fox's Bill on the law of libel; where, before passing the Bill, this House called on the Judges to give their opinions on what was the law as it then existed.

Lord Campbell:--My Lords, I cannot avoid expressing my satisfaction, that the noble and learned Lord on the woolsack carried into effect his desire to put these questions to the Judges. It was most fit that the opinions of the Judges should be asked on these matters, the settling of which is not a mere matter of speculation; for your Lordships may be called on, in your legislative capacity, to change the law; and before doing so, it is proper that you should be satisfied beyond doubt what the law really is. It is desirable to have such questions argued at the bar, but such a course is not always practicable. Your Lordships have been reminded of one precedent for this proceeding, but there is a still more recent instance; the Judges having been summoned in the case of the Canada Reserves, to express their opinions on what was then the law on that subject. The answers given by the Judges are most highly satisfactory, and will be of the greatest use in the administration of justice.

Lord Cottenham:--My Lords, I fully concur with the opinion now expressed, as to the obligations we owe to the Judges. It is true that they cannot be required to say what would be the construction of a Bill, not in existence as a law at the moment at which the question is put to them; but they may be called on to assist your Lordships, in declaring their opinions upon abstract questions of existing law.

Lord Wynford:--My Lords, I never doubted that your Lordships possess the power to call on the Judges to give their opinions upon questions of existing law, proposed to them as these questions have been. I myself recollect, that when I had the honour to hold the office of Lord Chief Justice of the Court of Common Pleas, I communicated to the House the opinions of the Judges on questions of this sort, framed with reference to the usury laws. Upon the opinion of the Judges thus delivered to the House by me, a Bill was founded, and afterwards passed into a law.

The Lord Chancellor:--My Lords, I entirely concur in the opinion given by my noble and learned friends, as to our right to have the opinions of the Judges on abstract questions of existing law; and I agree that we owe our thanks to the Judges, for the attention and learning with which they have answered the questions now put to them.

Discussion Question

Based upon the facts as related in this case (you are free to consult other sources as well), do you believe that the prisoner should have been found guilty or not guilty? Remember that in virtually every jurisdiction in the United States and throughout the British Commonwealth, the defense of insanity continues to exist and is based upon this case.

Critical Thinking Exercise

If you were tasked to develop recommendations on reform in the area of insanity to be included in the Model Penal Code, what might they be? List in outline form.

STATUTORY REFERENCES

By

John Robert Cencich, J.S.D.

YOU HAVE ALREADY HAD AN OPPORTUNITY TO BE introduced to the notion of insanity, particularly from a common law perspective. What follows are some references to specific criminal statutes that relate to individual criminal responsibility and the mental state of the accused. Indeed, you should use these references as you read the chapter on insanity and other medico-legal concepts.

For example, you should know that for any crime to exist there must be a concurrence of the *actus reus* (guilty act) and the *mens rea* (guilty mind). In other words, generally speaking this means that one who commits a physical act without the requisite intent or other form of guilty mind, e.g., negligence or recklessness, does not commit a crime. The opposite holds true as well. By this I mean one who would like to see a crime committed, e.g., the death of a spouse, does not commit a crime if the person did not commit or otherwise participate in the act.

These concepts become a bit more convoluted when we add the notion of criminal omission into the mix, and then on top of that, the mental state relative to the omission. For example, a criminal homicide can occur when a person fails to provide life-dependent care for their spouse, and consequently the analysis typically focuses on whether the spouse knew or should have known that they had such a duty. Furthermore, the question is also asked as to whether the actor knew or should have known that the failure to provide the care would cause death or grievous bodily harm. Much of this analysis is complicated further depending upon the jurisdiction as some apply objected standards while others employ subjective or even further, a combination of objective and subjective standards.

In any event, you should find these statutory references helpful in your own analysis throughout this course. I have broken these references into three jurisdictional groups. The first involves federal statutes, the second relate to the Commonwealth of Pennsylvania, and the last are based upon what is known as the Model Penal Code (MPC). The MPC was developed by the American Law Institute (ALI), and it serves to provide lawyers, students, scholars, legislators, and judges with the basic framework of how a particular criminal statute might be formulated. Please note that the MPC is not the law. It is being used for its intended purposes and due to the fact that it is impossible to cover the law of all states in this course. Nevertheless, the combination of these three sources should provide the reader with a good representation of relevant statutory law used throughout the United States.

Federal Statutes

Principals: 18 U.S.C. § 2
(a) Whoever commits an offense against the United States or aids, abets, counsels, commands, induces or procures its commission, is punishable as a principal.

(b) Whoever willfully causes an act to be done which if directly performed by him or another would be an offense against the United States, is punishable as a principal.

Accessory After the Fact: 18 U.S.C. § 3
Whoever, knowing that an offense against the United States has been committed, receives, relieves, comforts or assists the offender in order to hinder or prevent his apprehension, trial or punishment, is an accessory after the fact.

Except as otherwise expressly provided by any Act of Congress, an accessory after the fact shall be imprisoned not more than one-half the maximum term of imprisonment or (notwithstanding section 3571) fined not more than one-half the maximum fine prescribed for the punishment of the principal, or both; or if the principal is punishable by life imprisonment or death, the accessory shall be imprisoned not more than 15 years.

Insanity Defense: 18 U.S.C. § 17

(a)   Affirmative   Defense.— It   is   an   affirmative defense to a prosecution under any Federal statute that, at the time of the commission of the acts constituting the offense, the defendant, as a result of a severe mental disease or defect, was unable to appreciate the nature and quality or the wrongfulness of his acts. Mental disease or defect does not otherwise constitute a defense.

(b) Burden of Proof.— The defendant has the burden of proving the defense of insanity by clear and convincing evidence.

Notice of an Insanity Defense; mental Examination: Rule 12.2 of the Federal Rules of Criminal Procedure

(a) NOTICE OF AN INSANITY DEFENSE. A defendant who intends to assert a defense of insanity at the time of the alleged offense must so notify an attorney for the government in writing within the time provided for filing a pretrial motion, or at any later time the court sets, and file a copy of the notice with the clerk. A defendant who fails to do so cannot rely on an insanity defense. The court may, for good cause, allow the defendant to file the notice late, grant additional trial-preparation time, or make other appropriate orders.

(b) NOTICE OF EXPERT EVIDENCE OF A MENTAL CONDITION. If a defendant intends to introduce expert evidence relating to a mental disease or defect or any other mental condition of the defendant bearing on either (1) the issue of guilt or (2) the issue of punishment in a capital case, the defendant must— within the time provided for filing a pretrial motion or at any later time the court sets—notify an attorney for the government in writing of this intention and file a copy of the notice with the clerk. The court may, for good cause, allow the defendant to file the notice late, grant the parties additional trial-preparation time, or make other appropriate orders.

Pennsylvania Statutes

Title 18 P.C.S.A.

§ 301. Requirement of voluntary act.
(a) General rule.--A person is not guilty of an offense unless his liability is based on conduct which includes a voluntary act or the omission to perform an act of which he is physically capable.

(b) Omission as basis of liability.--Liability for the commission of an offense may not be based on an omission unaccompanied by action unless:

(1) the omission is expressly made sufficient by the law defining the offense; or

(2) a duty to perform the omitted act is otherwise imposed by law.

(c) Possession as an act.--Possession is an act, within the meaning of this section, if the possessor knowingly procured or received the thing possessed or was aware of his control thereof for a sufficient period to have been able to terminate his possession.

§ 302. General requirements of culpability.

(a) Minimum requirements of culpability.--Except as provided in section 305 of this title (relating to limitations on scope of culpability requirements), a person is not guilty of an offense unless he acted intentionally, knowingly, recklessly or negligently, as the law may require, with respect to each material element of the offense.

(b) Kinds of culpability defined.--

(1) A person acts intentionally with respect to a material element of an offense when:

(i) if the element involves the nature of his conduct or a result thereof, it is his conscious object to engage in conduct of that nature or to cause such a result; and

(ii) if the element involves the attendant circumstances, he is aware of the existence of such circumstances or he believes or hopes that they exist.

(2) A person acts knowingly with respect to a material element of an offense when:

(i) if the element involves the nature of his conduct or the attendant circumstances, he is aware that his conduct is of that nature or that such circumstances exist; and

(ii) if the element involves a result of his conduct, he is aware that it is practically certain that his conduct will cause such a result.

(3) A person acts recklessly with respect to a material element of an offense when he consciously disregards a substantial and unjustifiable risk that the material element exists or will result from his conduct. The risk must be of such a nature and degree that, considering the nature and intent of the actor's conduct and the circumstances known to him, its disregard involves a gross deviation from the standard of conduct that a reasonable person would observe in the actor's situation.

(4) A person acts negligently with respect to a material element of an offense when he should be aware of a substantial and unjustifiable risk that the material element exists or will result from his conduct. The risk must be of such a nature and degree that the actor's failure to perceive it, considering the nature and intent of his conduct and the circumstances known to him, involves a gross deviation from the standard of care that a reasonable person would observe in the actor's situation.

(c) Culpability required unless otherwise provided.- -When the culpability sufficient to establish a material element of an offense is not prescribed by law, such element is established if a person acts intentionally, knowingly or recklessly with respect thereto.

(d) Prescribed culpability requirement applies to all material elements.--When the law defining an offense prescribes the kind of culpability that is sufficient for the commission of an offense, without distinguishing among the material elements thereof, such provision shall apply to all the material elements of the offense, unless a contrary purpose plainly appears.

(e) Substitutes for negligence, recklessness and knowledge.--When the law provides that negligence suffices to establish an element of an offense, such element also is established if a person acts intentionally or knowingly. When acting knowingly suffices to establish an element, such element also is established if a person acts intentionally.

(f) Requirement of intent satisfied if intent is conditional.--When a particular intent is an element of an offense, the element is established although such intent is conditional, unless the condition negatives the harm or evil sought to be prevented by the law defining the offense.

(g) Requirement of willfulness satisfied by acting knowingly.--A requirement that an offense be committed willfully is satisfied if a person acts knowingly with respect to the material elements of the offense, unless a purpose to impose further requirements appears.

(h) Culpability as to illegality of conduct.--Neither knowledge nor recklessness or negligence as to whether conduct constitutes an offense or as to the existence, meaning or application of the law determining the elements of an offense is an element of such offense, unless the definition of the offense or this title so provides.

§ 303. Causal relationship between conduct and result.

(a) General rule.--Conduct is the cause of a result when:

(1) it is an antecedent but for which the result in question would not have occurred; and

(2) the relationship between the conduct and result satisfies any additional causal requirements imposed by this title or by the law defining the offense.

(b) Divergence between result designed or contemplated and actual result.--When intentionally or knowingly causing a particular result is an element of an offense, the element is not established if the actual result is not within the intent or the contemplation of the actor unless:

(1) the actual result differs from that designed or contemplated as the case may be, only in the respect

that a different person or different property is injured or affected or that the injury or harm designed or contemplated would have been more serious or more extensive than that caused; or

(2) the actual result involves the same kind of injury or harm as that designed or contemplated and is not too remote or accidental in its occurrence to have a bearing on the actor's liability or on the gravity of his offense.

(c) Divergence between probable and actual result.--When recklessly or negligently causing a particular result is an element of an offense, the element is not established if the actual result is not within the risk of which the actor is aware or, in the case of negligence, of which he should be aware unless:

(1) the actual result differs from the probable result only in the respect that a different person or different property is injured or affected or that the probable injury or harm would have been more serious or more extensive than that caused; or

(2) the actual result involves the same kind of injury or harm as the probable result and is not too remote or accidental in its occurrence to have a bearing on the liability of the actor or on the gravity of his offense.

(d) Absolute liability.--When causing a particular result is a material element of an offense for which absolute liability is imposed by law, the element is not established unless the actual result is a probable consequence of the conduct of the actor.

§ 304. Ignorance or mistake.

Ignorance or mistake as to a matter of fact, for which there is reasonable explanation or excuse, is a defense if:

(1) the ignorance or mistake negatives the intent, knowledge, belief, recklessness, or negligence required to establish a material element of the offense; or

(2) the law provides that the state of mind established by such ignorance or mistake constitutes a defense.

§ 305. Limitations on scope of culpability requirements.

(a) When culpability requirements are inapplicable to summary offenses and to offenses defined by other statutes.--The requirements of culpability prescribed by section 301 of this title (relating to requirement of voluntary act) and section 302 of this title (relating to general requirements of culpability) do not apply to:

(1) summary offenses, unless the requirement involved is included in the definition of the offense or the court determines that its application is consistent with effective enforcement of the law defining the offense; or
(2) offenses defined by statutes other than this title, in so far as a legislative purpose to impose absolute liability for such offenses or with respect to any material element thereof plainly appears.
(b) Effect of absolute liability in reducing grade of offense to summary offense.--Notwithstanding any other provision of existing law and unless a subsequent statute otherwise provides:
(1) when absolute liability is imposed with respect to any material element of an offense defined by a statute other than this title and a conviction is based upon such liability, the offense constitutes a summary offense; and
(2) although absolute liability is imposed by law with respect to one or more of the material elements of an offense defined by a statute other than this title, the culpable commission of the offense may be charged and proved, in which event negligence with respect to such elements constitutes sufficient culpability and the classification of the offense and the sentence that

may be imposed therefor upon conviction are determined by section 106 of this title (relating to classes of offenses) and Chapter 11 of this title (relating to authorized disposition of offenders).

§ 306. Liability for conduct of another; complicity.

(a) General rule.--A person is guilty of an offense if it is committed by his own conduct or by the conduct of another person for which he is legally accountable, or both.

(b) Conduct of another.--A person is legally accountable for the conduct of another person when:

(1) acting with the kind of culpability that is sufficient for the commission of the offense, he causes an innocent or irresponsible person to engage in such conduct;

(2) he is made accountable for the conduct of such other person by this title or by the law defining the offense; or

(3) he is an accomplice of such other person in the commission of the offense.

(c) Accomplice defined.--A person is an accomplice of another person in the commission of an offense if:

(1) with the intent of promoting or facilitating the commission of the offense, he:

(i) solicits such other person to commit it; or

(ii) aids or agrees or attempts to aid such other person in planning or committing it; or

(2) his conduct is expressly declared by law to establish his complicity.

(d) Culpability of accomplice.--When causing a particular result is an element of an offense, an accomplice in the conduct causing such result is an accomplice in the commission of that offense, if he acts with the kind of culpability, if any, with respect to that result that is sufficient for the commission of the offense.

(e) Status of actor.--In any prosecution for an offense in which criminal liability of the defendant is based upon the conduct of another person pursuant to this section, it is no defense that the offense in question, as defined, can be committed only by a particular class or classes of persons, and the defendant, not belonging to such class or classes, is for that reason legally incapable of committing the offense in an individual capacity.

(f) Exceptions.--Unless otherwise provided by this title or by the law defining the offense, a person is not an accomplice in an offense committed by another person if:

(1) he is a victim of that offense;

(2) the offense is so defined that his conduct is inevitably incident to its commission; or

(3) he terminates his complicity prior to the commission of the offense and:

(i) wholly deprives it of effectiveness in the commission of the offense; or

(ii) gives timely warning to the law enforcement authorities or otherwise makes proper effort to prevent the commission of the offense.

(g) Prosecution of accomplice only.--An accomplice may be convicted on proof of the commission of the offense and of his complicity therein, though the person claimed to have committed the offense has not been prosecuted or convicted or has been convicted of a different offense or degree of offense or has an immunity to prosecution or conviction or has been acquitted.

§ 307. Liability of organizations and certain related persons.

(a) Corporations generally.--A corporation may be convicted of the commission of an offense if:

(1) the offense is a summary offense or the offense is defined by a statute other than this title in which a legislative purpose to impose liability on corporations plainly appears and the conduct is performed by an agent of the corporation acting in behalf of the

corporation within the scope of his office or employment, except that if the law defining the offense designates the agents for whose conduct the corporation is accountable or the circumstances under which it is accountable, such provisions shall apply;

(2) the offense consists of an omission to discharge a specific duty of affirmative performance imposed on corporations by law; or

(3) the commission of the offense was authorized, requested, commanded, performed or recklessly tolerated by the board of directors or by a high managerial agent acting in behalf of the corporation within the scope of his office or employment.

(b) Corporations, absolute liability.--When absolute liability is imposed for the commission of an offense, a legislative purpose to impose liability on a corporation shall be assumed, unless the contrary plainly appears.

(c) Unincorporated associations.

--An unincorporated association may be convicted of the commission of an offense if:

(1) the offense is defined by a statute other than this title which expressly provides for the liability of such an association and the conduct is performed by an agent of the association acting in behalf of the association within the scope of his office or employment, except that if the law defining the offense designates the agents for whose conduct the association is accountable or the circumstances under which it is accountable, such provisions shall apply; or

(2) the offense consists of an omission to discharge a specific duty of affirmative performance imposed on associations by law.

(d) Defenses.--In any prosecution of a corporation or an unincorporated association for the commission of an offense included within the terms of paragraph (a)(1) or paragraph (c)(1) of this section, other than an offense for which absolute liability has been imposed, it shall be a defense if the defendant proves by a preponderance of evidence that the high managerial agent having supervisory responsibility over the subject matter of the offense employed due diligence to prevent its commission. This subsection shall not apply if it is plainly inconsistent with the legislative purpose in defining the particular offense.

(e) Persons acting or under a duty to act for organizations.--
(1) A person is legally accountable for any conduct he performs or causes to be performed in the name of a corporation or an unincorporated association or in its behalf to the same extent as if it were performed in his own name or behalf.

(2) Whenever a duty to act is imposed by law upon a corporation or an unincorporated association, any agent of the corporation or association having primary responsibility for the discharge of the duty is legally accountable for a reckless omission to perform the required act to the same extent as if the duty were imposed by law directly upon himself.

(3) When a person is convicted of an offense by reason of his legal accountability for the conduct of a corporation or an unincorporated association, he is subject to the sentence authorized by law when a natural person is convicted of an offense of the grade and the degree involved.

(f) Definitions.--As used in this section the following words and phrases shall have the meanings given to them in this subsection:

"Agent." Any director, officer, servant, employee or other person authorized to act in behalf of the corporation or association and, in the case of an unincorporated association, a member of such association.

"Corporation." Does not include an entity organized as or by a governmental agency for the execution of a governmental program.

"High managerial agent." An officer of a corporation or an unincorporated association, or, in the case of a partnership, a partner, or any other agent of a corporation or association having duties of such responsibility that his conduct may fairly be assumed to represent the policy of the corporation or association.

§ 308. Intoxication or drugged condition.

Neither voluntary intoxication nor voluntary drugged condition is a defense to a criminal charge, nor may evidence of such conditions be introduced to negative the element of intent of the offense, except that evidence of such intoxication or drugged condition of the defendant may be offered by the defendant whenever it is relevant to reduce murder from a higher degree to a lower degree of murder.

§ 309. Duress.

(a) General rule.--It is a defense that the actor engaged in the conduct charged to constitute an offense because he was coerced to do so by the use of, or a threat to use, unlawful force against his person or the person of another, which a person of reasonable firmness in his situation would have been unable to resist.

(b) Exception.--The defense provided by subsection (a) of this section is unavailable if the actor recklessly placed himself in a situation in which it was probable that he would be subjected to duress. The defense is also unavailable if he was negligent in placing himself in such a situation, whenever negligence suffices to establish culpability for the offense charged.

§ 310. Military orders.

It is a defense that the actor, in engaging in the conduct charged to constitute an offense, does no more than execute an order of his superior in the armed services which he does not know and cannot reasonably be expected to know to be unlawful.

§ 311. Consent.

(a) General rule.--The consent of the victim to conduct charged to constitute an offense or to the result thereof is a defense if such consent negatives an element of the offense or precludes the infliction of the harm or evil sought to be prevented by the law defining the offense.

(b) Consent to bodily injury.--When conduct is charged to constitute an offense because it causes or threatens bodily injury, consent to such conduct or to the infliction of such injury is a defense if:

(1) the conduct and the injury are reasonably foreseeable hazards of joint participation in a lawful athletic contest or competitive sport; or

(2) the consent establishes a justification for the conduct under Chapter 5 of this title (relating to general principles of justification).

(c) Ineffective consent.--Unless otherwise provided by this title or by the law defining the offense, assent does not constitute consent if:

(1) it is given by a person who is legally incapacitated to authorize the conduct charged to constitute the offense;

(2) it is given by a person who by reason of youth, mental disease or defect or intoxication is manifestly unable or known by the actor to be unable to make a reasonable judgment as to the nature or harmfulness of the conduct charged to constitute the offense;

(3) it is given by a person whose improvident consent is sought to be prevented by the law defining the offense; or

(4) it is induced by force, duress or deception of a kind sought to be prevented by the law defining the offense.

(Apr. 16, 1992, P.L.108, No.24, eff. 60 days)

§ 312. De minimis infractions.

(a) General rule.--The court shall dismiss a prosecution if, having regard to the nature of the conduct charged to constitute an offense and the nature of the attendant circumstances, it finds that the conduct of the defendant:

(1) was within a customary license or tolerance, neither expressly negatived by the person whose interest was infringed nor inconsistent with the purpose of the law defining the offense;

(2) did not actually cause or threaten the harm or evil sought to be prevented by the law defining the offense or did so only to an extent too trivial to warrant the condemnation of conviction; or

(3) presents such other extenuations that it cannot reasonably be regarded as envisaged by the General Assembly or other authority in forbidding the offense.

(b) Written statement.--The court shall not dismiss a prosecution under this section without filing a written statement of its reasons, except that if the attorney for the Commonwealth is the moving party for such dismissal no such written statement need be filed.

(June 22, 1978, P.L.494, No.73, eff. 60 days)

§ 313. Entrapment.

(a) General rule.--A public law enforcement official or a person acting in cooperation with such an official perpetrates an entrapment if for the purpose of obtaining evidence of the commission of an offense, he induces or encourages another person to engage in conduct constituting such offense by either:

(1) making knowingly false representations designed to induce the belief that such conduct is not prohibited; or

(2) employing methods of persuasion or inducement which create a substantial risk that such an offense will be committed by persons other than those who are ready to commit it.

(b) Burden of proof.--Except as provided in subsection (c) of this section, a person prosecuted for an offense shall be acquitted if he proves by a preponderance of evidence that his conduct occurred in response to an entrapment.

(c) Exception.--The defense afforded by this section is unavailable when causing or threatening bodily injury is an element of the offense charged and the prosecution is based on conduct causing or threatening such injury to a person other than the person perpetrating the entrapment.

§ 314. Guilty but mentally ill.

(a) General rule.--A person who timely offers a defense of insanity in accordance with the Rules of Criminal Procedure may be found "guilty but mentally ill" at trial if the trier of facts finds, beyond a reasonable doubt, that the person is guilty of an offense, was mentally ill at the time of the commission of the offense and was not legally insane at the time of the commission of the offense.

(b) Plea of guilty but mentally ill.--A person who waives his right to trial may plead guilty but mentally ill. No plea of guilty but mentally ill may be accepted by the trial judge until he has examined all reports prepared pursuant to the Rules of Criminal Procedure, has held a hearing on the sole issue of the defendant's mental illness at which either party may present evidence and is satisfied that the defendant was mentally ill at the time of the offense to which the plea is entered. If the trial judge refuses to accept a plea of guilty but mentally ill, the defendant shall be permitted to withdraw his plea. A defendant whose plea is not accepted by the court shall be entitled to a jury trial, except that if a defendant subsequently waives his right to a jury trial, the judge who presided at the hearing on mental illness shall not preside at the trial.

(c) Definitions.--For the purposes of this section and 42 Pa.C.S. § 9727 (relating to disposition of persons found guilty but mentally ill):

(1) "Mentally ill." One who as a result of mental disease or defect, lacks substantial capacity either to appreciate the wrongfulness of his conduct or to conform his conduct to the requirements of the law.

(2) "Legal insanity." At the time of the commission of the act, the defendant was laboring under such a defect of reason, from disease of the mind, as not to know the nature and quality of the act he was doing or, if he did know it, that he did not know he was doing what was wrong.

(d) Common law M'Naghten's Rule preserved.-- Nothing in this section shall be deemed to repeal or otherwise abrogate the common law defense of insanity (M'Naghten's Rule) in effect in this Commonwealth on the effective date of this section.

§ 315. Insanity.

(a) General rule.--The mental soundness of an actor engaged in conduct charged to constitute an offense shall only be a defense to the charged offense when the actor proves by a preponderance of evidence that the actor was legally insane at the time of the commission of the offense.

(b) Definition.--For purposes of this section, the phrase "legally insane" means that, at the time of the commission of the offense, the actor was laboring under such a defect of reason, from disease of the mind, as not to know the nature and quality of the act he was doing or, if the actor did know the quality of the act, that he did not know that what he was doing was wrong.

Model Penal Code

Article 2 General Principles of Liability

§ 2.01. Requirement of Voluntary Act; Omission as Basis of Liability; Possession as an Act.

(1) A person is not guilty of an offense unless his liability is based on conduct that includes a voluntary act or the omission to perform an act of which he is physically capable.

(2) The following are not voluntary acts within the meaning of this Section:

(a)   a reflex or convulsion;

(b)   a bodily movement during unconsciousness or sleep;

(c)   conduct during hypnosis or resulting from hypnotic suggestion;

(d)   a bodily movement that otherwise is not a product of the effort or determination of the actor, either conscious or habitual.

(3)   Liability for the commission of an offense may not be based on an omission unaccompanied by action unless:

(a)   the omission is expressly made sufficient by the law defining the offense; or

(b)   a duty to perform the omitted act is otherwise imposed by law.

(4) Possession is an act, within the meaning of this Section, if the possessor knowingly procured or received the thing possessed or was aware of his control thereof for a sufficient period to have been able to terminate his possession.

§ 2.02. General Requirements of Culpability.

(1) Minimum Requirements of Culpability. Except as provided in Section 2.05, a person is not guilty of an offense unless he acted purposely, knowingly, recklessly or negligently, as the law may require, with respect to each material element of the offense.

(2)   Kinds of Culpability Defined.

(a)   Purposely.

A person acts purposely with respect to a material element of an offense when:

(i)   if the element involves the nature of his conduct or a result thereof, it is his conscious object to engage in conduct of that nature or to cause such a result; and

(ii) if the element involves the attendant circumstances, he is aware of the existence of such circumstances or he believes or hopes that they exist.

(b)   Knowingly.

A person acts knowingly with respect to a material element of an offense when:

(i)   if the element involves the nature of his conduct or the attendant circumstances, he is aware that his conduct is of that nature or that such circumstances exist; and

(ii)   if the element involves a result of his conduct, he is aware that it is practically certain that his conduct will cause such a result.

(c)   Recklessly.

A person acts recklessly with respect to a material element of an offense when he consciously disregards a substantial and unjustifiable risk that the material element exists or will result from his conduct. The risk must be of such a nature and degree that, considering the nature and purpose of the actor's conduct and the circumstances known to him, its disregard involves a gross deviation from the standard of conduct that a law-abiding person would observe in the actor's situation.

(d)   Negligently.

A person acts negligently with respect to a material element of an offense when he should be aware of a substantial and unjustifiable risk that the material element exists or will result from his conduct.

The risk must be of such a nature and degree that the actor's failure to perceive it, considering the nature and purpose of his conduct and the circumstances known to him, involves a gross deviation from the standard of care that a reasonable person would observe in the actor's situation.

(3) Culpability Required Unless Otherwise Provided. When the culpability sufficient to establish a material element of an offense is not prescribed by law, such element is established if a person acts purposely, knowingly or recklessly with respect thereto.

(4) Prescribed Culpability Requirement Applies to All Material Elements. When the law defining an offense prescribes the kind of culpability that is sufficient for the commission of an offense, without distinguishing

among the material elements thereof, such provision shall apply to all the material elements of the offense, unless a contrary purpose plainly appears.

(5) Substitutes for Negligence, Recklessness and Knowledge. When the law provides that negligence suffices to establish an element of an offense, such element also is established if a person acts purposely, knowingly or recklessly. When recklessness suffices to establish an element, such element also is established if a person acts purposely or knowingly. When acting knowingly suffices to establish an element, such element also is established if a person acts purposely.

(6) Requirement of Purpose Satisfied if Purpose Is Conditional. When a particular purpose is an element of an offense, the element is established although such purpose is conditional, unless the condition negatives the harm or evil sought to be prevented by the law defining the offense.

(7) Requirement of Knowledge Satisfied by Knowledge of High Probability. When knowledge of the existence of a particular fact is an element of an offense, such knowledge is established if a person is aware of a high probability of its existence, unless he actually believes that it does not exist.

(8) Requirement of Wilfulness Satisfied by Acting Knowingly. A requirement that an offense be committed wilfully is satisfied if a person acts knowingly with respect to the material elements of the offense, unless a purpose to impose further requirements appears.

(9) Culpability as to Illegality of Conduct. Neither knowledge nor recklessness or negligence as to

whether conduct constitutes an offense or as to the existence, meaning or application of the law determining the elements of an offense is an element of such offense, unless the definition of the offense or the Code so provides.

(10)   Culpability as Determinant of Grade of Offense. When the grade or degree of an offense depends on whether the offense is committed purposely, knowingly, recklessly or negligently, its grade or degree shall be the lowest for which the determinative kind of culpability is established with respect to any material element of the offense.

§ 4.02. Evidence of Mental Disease or Defect Admissible

When Relevant to Element of the Offense [Mental Disease or Defect Impairing Capacity as Ground for Mitigation of Punishment in Capital Cases].

(1) Evidence that the defendant suffered from a mental disease or defect is admissible whenever it is relevant to prove that the defendant did or did not have a state of mind that is an element of the offense.

(2) Whenever the jury or the Court is authorized to determine or to recommend whether or not the defendant shall be sentenced to death or imprisonment upon conviction, evidence that the capacity of the defendant to appreciate the criminality [wrongfulness] of his conduct or to conform his conduct to the requirements of law was impaired as a result of mental disease or defect is admissible in favor of sentence of imprisonment.

Discussion Question

Based upon the information contained in the three sources of statutory framework, which do you believe presents the best balance in terms of fairness to the suspect and the public?

Critical Thinking Exercise

If you had to make a recommendation from a legislative standpoint concerning the defense of insanity and the disposition of guilty but mentally ill, what factors (in outline form) do you think should be considered?

Focus on Psychopathy

Reprinted from July 2012
FBI Law Enforcement Bulletin

PSYCHOPATHY IS A WELL-KNOWN CONCEPT IN THE discussion of criminal behavior. Members of the law enforcement community, media, and general public often quickly label an individual a psychopath when hearing tales of violent crime, serial killing, financial scandal, and public corruption. While people must take caution when labeling someone too hastily based on limited information, officers find investigative value in identifying behavior indicative of psychopathy. Quite simply, they can combat crime more effectively when knowing the offender.

Although associated with aggressive and antisocial actions, psychopathy differs, in general, from criminal behavior. Not all psychopaths are criminals. However, some are, and their criminal behavior is predatory in nature. People often describe these individuals as charming, manipulative, and without conscience. Although they make up only 1 percent or so of the general population, psychopaths commit a disproportionate amount of serious and violent crime. This illustrates why identifying psychopathic behavior proves critical to an investigator's mission.

Knowing and understanding an offender's personality traits can help officers develop appropriate strategies for complex and unusual investigations. To this end, comprehending an offender's psychopathy becomes critical in a serial murder, rape, or child abduction case. Crime scene and postoffense behavior of the psychopath likely will differ from that of nonpsychopaths committing similar offenses. These differences can help law enforcement link serial investigations. While preparing interview strategies, investigators benefit when they recognize their offender as a psychopath because certain themes may prove unsuccessful. While psychopaths present challenges to officers, they also possess personality traits that law enforcement can exploit successfully.

A clear and concise discussion of psychopathy can lead to a greater understanding of the challenges associated with these offenders. Further, this knowledge can promote and enhance cooperation between law enforcement entities to successfully combat the devastating effects criminal psychopaths have on society. To this end, the FBI can offer assistance and expertise.

Part of the Critical Incident Response Group, three Behavioral Analysis Units (BAUs) provide investigative and operational support to federal, state, local, and international law enforcement agencies through the application of investigative experience, training, and research. BAU resources have focused on unusual or repetitive cases of violent crime, such as sexual assault and serial, mass, and other murder; kidnapping; child abduction; missing persons; communicated threats; terrorist acts; public corruption; white collar offenses; and cyber crime.
The Training Division's Behavioral Science Unit (BSU) provides education in various topics in the behavioral sciences to law enforcement executives from around the world who attend the FBI's National Academy.

Instructors also train new FBI agents, onboard employees, and state and local law enforcement partners through road schools across the country. In addition to their teaching duties, BSU members conduct research, host conferences, and write articles for publication on topics of importance to law enforcement to advance the field of knowledge in the behavioral sciences.

Timothy Slater, Unit Chief, Behavioral Analysis Unit 2, Critical Incident Response Group, Federal Bureau of Investigation.

Lydia Pozzato, Special Agent, Behavioral Science Unit, Training Division, Federal Bureau of Investigation

I am honored by the invitation to write an introduction to this focus issue of the *FBI Law Enforcement Bulletin.* I have spent my career conducting basic and applied research on psychopathy, a vitally important clinical construct. The academic view of psychopathy resonates seamlessly with those who work in the criminal justice system and routinely encounter people who embody the traits and behaviors that define this condition.

Psychopaths—perhaps 1 percent of the general population and 10 to 15 percent of offenders—are manipulative, deceptive, self-centered, lacking in empathy and guilt, callous, and remorseless. They present a serious challenge to everyone involved with criminal justice, including officers and investigators; judges, prosecutors, and defense attorneys; probation officers; corrections personnel; and psychologists, psychiatrists, and social workers. For more than three decades, I have had the pleasure of discussing the nature and implications of psychopathy with these groups. But, I derive particular satisfaction from working with those in the front line of law enforcement because they must face head-on the likelihood that some of the people with whom they deal are psychopathic. The consequences of these encounters always are uncertain and sometimes dangerous.

Most law enforcement officers learn quickly about the varieties and vagaries of human nature, and many have the experience and intuitive skills needed to guide their evaluations and interactions with the public. On the other hand, it is not uncommon for even the most astute officers to operate under the mistaken belief that others think and feel much as they do and to become the target of manipulation by one who is more skilled at playing head games. When officers do not know or suspect psychopathy during first contacts with individuals, the results can prove deadly, as Anthony Pinizzotto, Edward Davis, and Charles Miller III first showed in their 1992 publication *Killed in the Line of Duty: A Study of Selected Felonious Killings of Law Enforcement Officers.*[1] This also can prove problematic during criminal investigations, undercover work, hostage negotiations, and interrogations, in which assumptions about the personality of a suspect may help determine strategies and tactics. In cases that involve white-collar crime, investigators also may feel frustrated and helpless when dealing with a system that seems to favor or fail to recognize the manipulative skills of psychopaths.

While welcome, the dramatic increase in awareness of the importance of psychopathy to the criminal justice system brings with it the need for caution. The emergence of media and other "experts" with little relevant formal training or experience has accompanied the popularity of movies and television dramas featuring criminal investigation and profiling. Unfortunately, the same holds true with respect to psychopathy and law enforcement. Authorities need to understand and refer to psychopathy properly, and those who provide training and consultation on the implications of psychopathy for law enforcement must have the credentials to do so. However, while qualified clinicians hold the responsibility for the *formal* assessment of psychopathy, those in law enforcement should continue to use their training, experience, and knowledge of psychopathy to generate hypotheses about the individuals they encounter. Simply recognizing that the behaviors and inferred traits of an individual seem consistent with psychopathy may prove useful in identifying effective investigative and interviewing strategies. In some cases, these informal impressions and evaluations may lead to requests for clinical assessments.

Over the years, I have had the honor and privilege of interacting and working with many outstanding experts in the FBI's Behavioral Analysis Unit and at the FBI Academy. Many have contributed to this focus issue, which realizes a dream that retired Supervisory Special Agent Mary Ellen O'Toole, Special Agent George DeShazor, and I had a decade or so ago. We thank the staff of the *FBI Law Enforcement Bulletin* for helping make this material available to the law enforcement community. I hope that the articles and information contained herein will motivate readers to dig more deeply into the theory and research on psychopathy. An up-to-date and downloadable list of publications on the topic is maintained at my website *http://www.hare.org.*

Endnotes
[1] Available from the Uniform Crime Reporting Program Office, FBI Complex, 1000 Custer Hollow Road, Clarksburg, WV 26206-0150 or by calling 888-827-6427 or 304-625-4995.

Dr. Robert Hare, professor of psychology, University of British Columbia, Vancouver, Canada

Discussion Question

The author discusses the fact that not all psychopaths engage in criminal behavior. Based up the sources in your primary textbook, as well as this article, where do you think the line is drawn between psychopaths who engage in criminal behaviour and those that do not?

Psychopathy:
An Important Forensic Concept
for the 21st Century

By

Paul Babiak, M.S., Ph.D.; Jorge Folino, M.D., Ph.D.;
Jeffrey Hancock, Ph.D.; Robert D. Hare, Ph.D.;
Matthew Logan, Ph.D., M.Ed.;
Elizabeth Leon Mayer, Ph.D.;
J. Reid Meloy, Ph.D.;
Helinä Häkkänen-Nyholm, Ph.D.;
Mary Ellen O'Toole, Ph.D.; Anthony Pinizzotto, Ph.D.;
Stephen Porter, Ph.D.; Sharon Smith, Ph.D.;
and Michael Woodworth, Ph.D.

Reprinted from the July 2012
FBI Law Enforcement Bulletin

OVER THE YEARS, HOLLYWOOD HAS PROVIDED MANY examples of psychopaths. As a result, psychopaths often are identified as scary people who look frightening or have other off-putting characteristics. In reality, a psychopath can be anyone—a neighbor, coworker, or homeless person. Each of these seemingly harmless people may prey continually on others around them.

Psychopathy and Personality Disorder

The term *psychopathy* refers to a personality disorder that includes a cluster of interpersonal, affective, lifestyle, and antisocial traits and behaviors.[1] These involve deception; manipulation; irresponsibility; impulsivity; stimulation seeking; poor behavioral controls; shallow affect; lack of empathy, guilt, or remorse; sexual promiscuity; callous disregard for the rights of others; and unethical and antisocial behaviors.[2]

Psychopathy is the most dangerous of the personality disorders. To understand it, one must know some fundamental principles about personality. Individuals' personalities represent who they are; they result from genetics and upbringing and reflect how persons view the world and think the world views them. Personalities dictate how people interact with others and how they cope with problems, both real and imagined. Individuals' personalities develop and evolve until approximately their late 20s, after which they are well-hardwired in place, unable to be altered.

Traits and Characteristics

Psychopathy is apparent in a specific cluster of traits and characteristics. These traits, ultimately, define adult psychopathy and begin to manifest themselves in early childhood.[3] The lifelong expression of this disorder is a product of complex interactions between biological and temperamental predispositions and social forces—in other words, the ways in which nature and nurture shape and define each other.[4]

Many psychopaths exhibit a profound lack of remorse for their aggressive actions, both violent and nonviolent, along with a corresponding lack of empathy for their victims. This central psychopathic concept enables them to act in a cold-blooded manner, using those around them as pawns to achieve goals and satisfy needs and desires, whether sexual, financial, physical, or emotional. Most psychopaths are grandiose, selfish sensation seekers who lack a moral compass—a conscience—and go through life taking what they want. They do not accept responsibility for their actions and find a way to shift the blame to someone or something else.

Chameleons and Predators

In general, psychopaths are glib and charming, and they use these attributes to manipulate others into trusting and believing in them. This may lead to people giving them money, voting them into office, or, possibly, being murdered by them. Because of their interpersonal prowess, most psychopaths can present themselves favorably on a first impression, and many function successfully in society.

Many of the attitudes and behaviors of psychopaths have a distinct predatory quality to them. Psychopaths see others as either competitive predators or prey. To understand how psychopaths achieve their goals, it is important to see them as classic predators. For instance, they surf the Internet looking for attractive persons to con or, even, murder and target retirees to charm them out of their life savings for a high-risk investment scam, later blaming them for being too trusting. Most psychopaths are skilled at camouflage through deception and manipulation, as well as stalking and locating areas where there is an endless supply of victims.[5] The psychopath is an intraspecies predator, and peoples' visceral reaction to them—"they made the hair stand up on my neck"—is an early warning system driven by fear of being prey to a predator.[6]

The psychopath's egocentricity and need for power and control are the perfect ingredients for a lifetime of antisocial and criminal activity. The ease with which a psychopath can engage in violence holds significance for society and law enforcement. Often, psychopaths are shameless in their actions against others, whether it is murdering someone in a calculated, cold-blooded manner, manipulating law enforcement during an interview, or claiming remorse for actions, but blaming the victim for the crime. This particularly proves true in cases involving sexual offenders who are psychopathic.

If psychopaths commit a homicide, their killing likely will be planned and purposeful, not the result of a loss of emotional control; their motive more commonly will involve sadistic gratification.[7] When faced with overwhelming evidence of their guilt, they frequently will claim they lost control or were in a rage when committing the act of violence. In fact, their violence often is emotionless, calculated, and completely controlled.[8] If psychopaths commit a serious crime with another individual (almost always a nonpsychopath), they often will avoid culpability by using the other individual to take the blame for the offense. Evidence suggests that this particular strategy is even more evident in serious multiple-perpetrator offences committed by a psychopathic youth with a nonpsychopathic partner.[9]

Myth Busting

Many misconceptions about psychopaths can lead to mistakes in investigations, interviews, and court proceedings. Psychopaths are both male and female, but more men are psychopaths than women. They represent all races, cultures, and socioeconomic backgrounds. Some are intelligent, while others possess average or below-average intelligence. They come from both single- and two-parent households and may themselves be married with children.

Psychopaths understand right from wrong. They know they are subject to society's rules, but willingly disregard them to pursue their own interests. They also are not out of touch with reality. They rarely become psychotic unless they also have a separate mental illness or use powerful drugs, such as stimulants. These hallmarks of genuine mental illness might be proposed during a criminal defense, but they often are successfully challenged at trial. Although usually manageable, psychopathy is not curable.

Presence In Society
Many psychopaths have little difficulty joining the ranks of business, politics, law enforcement, government, and academia.[10] They exist in all lines of work, from executive to blue-collar professions. However, psychopathy often is misread, misdiagnosed, minimized, or explained away by professionals whose jobs require regular interaction with psychopaths, namely in the mental health, judicial, and law enforcement communities. When these professionals encounter psychopathy in the course of their work, their reaction and response to the psychopath may be too little and too late. Their lack of information can lead to serious consequences, ranging from mishandling the strategy for interviews and interrogations to believing a psychopath's complete fabrications as seemingly plausible explanations.

Assessment Tool
Following on approximately 40 years of empirical research, the Psychopathy Checklist-Revised, or PCL-R, has emerged as an ideal tool for the assessment of this personality disorder. Specific scoring criteria rate each of 20 items on a 3-point scale (0, 1, 2) according to the extent that it applies to a given individual. This test allows for a maximum score of 40; a score of 30 designates someone as a psychopath. The average nonpsychopath will score around 5 or 6 on this test.

White-collar or corporate psychopaths likely will score lower—in the middle 20s—and sexually deviant psychopaths will tend to score higher.[11]

Psychopaths differ from each other, and their condition can vary in severity. Current research suggests a continuum of psychopathy ranging from those who are highly psychopathic to persons who have the same number or fewer traits in a milder form. A clinical assessment of psychopathy is based on the person having the full cluster of psychopathic traits— at least to some degree—based on a pattern of lifetime behaviors.

Many psychopaths are not violent. However, those who display violence and sexual deviance are generally more dangerous than other offenders, and their likelihood of reoffending may be significantly higher.[12] Psychopaths tend to have longer, more varied, and more serious criminal histories and, overall, are more consistently violent than nonpsychopaths. Their use of violence appears to be less situational and more directed toward particular goals than the type of violence displayed by nonpsychopaths.[13] It is estimated that approximately 1 percent of the general male population are psychopaths, and 15 to 20 percent of the prison population are psychopathic.[14]

Given the risk that psychopathic offenders pose for society, their ability to potentially manipulate the authorities poses concern. Psychopathic killers more likely will deny charges brought against them, and some indication exists that they are able to manipulate the criminal justice system to receive reduced sentences and appeal sentences to a higher court.[15] Also, psychopathic sex offenders are 2.43 times more likely to be released than their nonpsychopathic counterparts, while psychopathic offenders charged with other crimes are 2.79 times more likely to be released.[16] Their acting ability can enable them to frequently manipulate and persuade members of a parole board to release them approximately 2.5 times faster than other offenders up for parole, despite their longer list of offenses and elevated risk.[17] Psychopaths can be adept at imitating emotions that they believe will mitigate their punishment.[18]

Research suggests that the linguistic patterns of psychopaths are unique compared with the patterns of nonpsychopaths. Their stylistic differences reflect how they view the world around them, as well as their profound emotional deficit and detachment from emotional events.[19] However, psychopaths' lack of feeling and bonding to others allows them to have clarity in observing the behavior of their prey. They do not get caught in or bogged down by the anxieties and emotions that other people experience in social situations.

Victims
The reactions of psychopaths to the damage they inflict most likely will be cool indifference and a sense of power, pleasure, or smug satisfaction, rather than regret or concern. Most people closely associated with a psychopath may know something is wrong with that person, but have no idea as to the depth of the pathology. They frequently will blame themselves for all of the problems they have had with a psychopath, whether at work, in a relationship, or within a family. After interacting with psychopaths, most people are stunned by these individuals' ruthlessness, callousness, and denial or minimization of the damage they have caused.

Conclusion
Psychopathy is not a diagnosis. About one-third of individuals in prison deemed "antisocial personality disordered," the current official Diagnostic and

Statistical Manual of Mental Disorders (DSM) diagnosis for the chronically antisocial, will meet the criteria for severe psychopathy. In DSM's upcoming fifth edition, psychopathy will become one of five dimensions for describing a personality disorder, receiving the official diagnostic blessing of American psychiatry after approximately one-half century of research.

Understanding the minds of psychopaths and their personality and behavioral traits allows authorities to design strategies that more likely will work with them. Psychopaths' manipulative nature can make it difficult for officers to obtain accurate information from them unless the law enforcement interviewer has been educated in specific strategies for questioning a psychopath. Professionals working in law enforcement, corrections, and other security-related professions must understand psychopathy and its implications.

Psychopathy has been described as the single most important clinical construct in the criminal justice system.[20] More recently, it is considered "the most important forensic concept of the early 21st century."[21] Because of its relevance to law enforcement, corrections, the courts, and others working in related fields, the need to understand psychopathy cannot be overstated. This includes knowing how to identify psychopaths, the damage they can cause, and how to deal with them more effectively.

Endnotes

[1] Robert D. Hare and Matthew H. Logan, "Criminal Psychopathy: An Introduction for Police," in *The Psychology of Criminal Investigations: The Search for the Truth*, ed. Michel St-Yves and Michel Tanguay (Cowansville, QC: Editions Yvon Blais, 2009).

[2] Hare and Logan, "Criminal Psychopathy: An Introduction for Police."

[3] Paul J. Frick and Monica A. Marsee, "Psychopathy and Developmental Pathways to Antisocial Behavior in Youth," in *Handbook of Psychopathy*, ed. Christopher J. Patrick (New York, NY: Guilford Press, 2006), 353-374; and Donald R. Lynam, "Early Identification of Chronic Offenders: Who is the Fledgling Psychopath?"*Psychological Bulletin* 120, no. 2 (1996): 209-234.

[4] Angus W. MacDonald III and William G. Iacono, "Toward an Integrated Perspective on the Etiology of Psychopathy," in *Handbook of Psychopathy*, ed. Christopher J. Patrick (New York, NY: Guilford Press, 2006), 375-385.

[5] Dewey G. Cornell, Janet Warren, Gary Hawk, Ed Stafford, Guy Oram, and Denise Pine, "Psychopathy in Instrumental and Reactive Violent Offenders," *Journal of Consulting and Clinical Psychology* 64, no. 4 (August 1996): 783-790; J. Reid Meloy, *The Psychopathic Mind: Origins, Dynamics, and Treatment*(Northvale, NJ: Jason Aronson, 1988); and Michael Woodworth and Stephen Porter, "In Cold Blood: Characteristics of Criminal Homicides as a Function of Psychopathy," *Journal of Abnormal Psychology* 111, no. 3 (2002): 436-445.

[6] J. Reid Meloy and M.J. Meloy, "Autonomic Arousal in the Presence of Psychopathy: A Survey of Mental Health and Criminal Justice Professionals," *Journal of Threat Assessment* 2, no.2 (2002): 21-34.

[7] Meloy, *The Psychopathic Mind: Origins, Dynamics, and Treatment*; and Stephen Porter and Michael Woodworth, "Psychopathy and Aggression," in *Handbook of Psychopathy*, ed. Christopher J. Patrick (New York, NY: Guilford Press, 2006), 481-494.

[8] Mary Ellen O'Toole, "Psychopathy as a Behavior Classification System for Violent and Serial Crime Scenes," in *The Psychopath: Theory, Research, and Practice*, ed. Hugues Hervé and John C. Yuille (Mahwah, NJ: Lawrence Erlbaum and Associates, 2007), 301-325; and Woodworth and Porter, "In Cold Blood: Characteristics of Criminal Homicides as a Function of Psychopathy."

[9] Woodworth and Porter, "In Cold Blood: Characteristics of Criminal Homicides as a Function of Psychopathy."

[10] Paul Babiak, "When Psychopaths Go to Work," *Applied Psychology: An International Review* 44, no. 2 (1995):171-188; and Paul Babiak and Robert D. Hare, *Snakes in Suits:*

When Psychopaths Go to Work(New York, NY: Harper/Collins, 2006).

[11] Robert D. Hare, *Hare Psychopathy Checklist-Revised,* 2nd ed. (Toronto, ON: Multi-Health Systems, 2003); and Babiak and Hare, *Snakes in Suits: When Psychopaths Go to Work.*

[12] Grant T. Harris, Marnie E. Rice, Vernon L. Quinsey, Martin L. Lalumière, Douglas Boer, and Carol Lang, "A Multisite Comparison of Actuarial Risk Instruments for Sex Offenders," *Psychological Assessment* 15, no. 3 (2003): 413-425.

[13] Stephen Porter, Leanne ten Brinke, and Kevin Wilson, "Crime Profiles and Conditional Release Performance of Psychopathic and Nonpsychopathic Sexual Offenders," *Legal and Criminological Psychology* 14, no. 1 (February 2009): 109-118.

[14] Robert D. Hare, "Psychopaths and Their Nature: Implications for the Mental Health and Criminal Justice Systems," in *Psychopathy: Antisocial, Criminal, and Violent Behavior,* ed. Theodore Millon, Erik Simonsen, Morten Birket-Smith, and Roger D. Davis (New York, NY: Guilford Press, 1998), 188-212.

[15] Helinä Häkkänen-Nyholm and Robert D. Hare, "Psychopathy, Homicide, and the Courts: Working the System," *Criminal Justice and Behavior* 36, no. 8 (2009): 761-777.

[16] Porter, ten Brinke, and Wilson, "Crime Profiles and Conditional Release Performance of Psychopathic and Nonpsychopathic Sexual Offenders."

[17] Porter, ten Brinke, and Wilson, "Crime Profiles and Conditional Release Performance of Psychopathic and Nonpsychopathic Sexual Offenders."

[18] Meloy, *The Psychopathic Mind: Origins, Dynamics, and Treatment.*

[19] Robert D. Hare, "Psychopathy, Affect, and Behavior," in *Psychopathy: Theory, Research, and Implications for Society,* ed. David J. Cooke, Adelle E. Forth, and Robert D. Hare (Dordrecht, The Netherlands: Kluwer, 1998), 105-137.

[20] Robert D. Hare, "Psychopathy: A Clinical Construct Whose Time Has Come," *Criminal Justice and Behavior* 23, no. 1 (March 1996): 25-54.

[21] John Monahan, comments on cover jacket of *Handbook of Psychopathy,* ed. Christopher J. Patrick (New York, NY: Guilford Press, 2006).

About the Authors

Dr. Babiak is a business author, international speaker, and consultant to executives and organizations on leadership development issues and the corporate psychopath.

Dr. Folino is a professor of psychiatry at the National University of La Plata, Argentina.

Dr. Hancock is an associate professor at Cornell University in Ithaca, New York.

Dr. Hare is a professor emeritus of psychology at the University of British Columbia, Vancouver, and a psychopathy researcher.

Dr. Logan, a retired staff sergeant with the Royal Canadian Mounted Police and a psychologist, provides forensic behavioral consultation and training for the law enforcement and criminal justice communities.

Dr. Mayer is a member of the psychiatric department at the National University of La Plata, Argentina.

Dr. Meloy is a consultant, researcher, writer, and teacher. He serves as a faculty member with the University of California, San Diego, School of Medicine and the San Diego Psychoanalytic Institute.

Dr. Häkkänen-Nyholm, a profiler at the Finnish National Bureau of Investigation, currently is the CEO of a psychology and law firm.

Dr. O'Toole has served with the FBI's Behavioral Analysis Unit and is a private forensic behavioral consultant and an instructor at the FBI Academy.

Dr. Pinizzotto, a retired FBI senior scientist, is a clinical forensic psychologist who privately consults for law enforcement and other criminal justice agencies.

Dr. Porter is a professor of psychology and the founding director of the Centre for the Advancement of Psychological Science and Law at the University of British Columbia, Okanangan.

Dr. Smith, a retired special agent with the FBI's Behavioral Science Unit, is a consultant on criminal and corporate psychopathy for intelligence- and security-related government and law enforcement agencies.

Dr. Woodworth is a registered psychologist and an associate professor at the University of British Columbia, Okanagan.

Critical Thinking Exercise

Using any resources available, in outline form discuss methods of identifying psychopaths among us.

THE LANGUAGE OF PSYCHOPATHS
NEW FINDINGS AND IMPLICATIONS FOR LAW ENFORCEMENT

By

Michael Woodworth, Ph.D.; Jeffrey Hancock, Ph.D.;
Stephen Porter, Ph.D.; Robert Hare, Ph.D.;
Matt Logan, Ph.D.; Mary Ellen O'Toole, Ph.D.;
and Sharon Smith, Ph.D.

Reprinted from July 2012
FBI Law Enforcement Bulletin

FOR PSYCHOPATHS, NOT ONLY A LACK OF AFFECT BUT ALSO inappropriate emotion may reveal the extent of their callousness. Recent research suggested that much can be learned about these individuals by close examination of their language. Their highly persuasive nonverbal behavior often distracts the listener from identifying their psychopathic nature.[1] For example, on a publically available police interview with murderer and rapist Paul Bernardo, his powerful use of communication via his hand gesturing is easily observable and often distracts from his spoken lies.[2] The authors offer their insights into the unique considerations pertaining to psychopaths' communication.

Psychopathy
Robert Pickton, convicted of the second-degree murder of six women in December 2007, initially was on trial

for 26 counts of first-degree murder. He once bragged to a cellmate that he intended to kill 50 women. Details provided in court revealed brutal and heinous murders that often included torture, degradation, and dismemberment of the victims. The authors opine that Mr. Pickton probably would meet the criteria for psychopathy, a destructive personality disorder that combines a profound lack of conscience with several problematic interpersonal, emotional, and behavioral characteristics.

Consistent with psychopathy, Robert Pickton's self-report and presentation during his interrogation showed a man devoid of emotion. His demeanor during this lengthy questioning reflected detachment and boredom. During most of his trial, Mr. Pickton was described as emotionless. Individuals present in court expressed dismay over his lack of emotion during the reading of horrifying impact statements.

With the nonchalant and emotionless demeanor of a psychopath, Robert Pickton would make an interesting case study. Reviewing his videotaped self-report with the sound muted, it appeared that he was reporting some mundane incident, rather than detailed accounts of the heinous murders he committed.

A psychopath recently interviewed by one of the authors recounted a vicious murder he had committed. "We got, uh, we got high, and had a few beers. I like whiskey, so I bought some whiskey, we had some of that, and then we, uh, went for a swim, and then we made love in my car, then we left to go get some more, some more booze and some more drugs." A recent study explained how this narrative might reveal important information regarding the mindset of a psychopath.[3]

Conning, manipulation, and a desire to lie for the sake of getting away with it—often referred to as "duping delight"—are well known characteristics of the psychopath. These behaviors, combined with a self-confident swagger and ability to distract the listener with grandiose self-presentation, make it difficult to properly follow their self-report.

Analysis and Technology
Individuals' language is one of the best ways to glean insight into their thoughts and general outlook. Recent advances in technology make it possible to examine more closely the language of various clinical populations through automatic linguistic analysis programs. These applications can differentiate between a variety of individual and personality factors.[4] The tools range from simple to sophisticated, but they all essentially identify linguistic patterns and count their frequency relative to a control language.

Considering the speech of narcissists, they use language related to the self more than nonnarcissistic people because of their primary concern with themselves. To analyze this, a program could count the number of times the words "I," "me," or "my" occurred in a person's speech and compare that to the general population. A narcissist's speech should have a higher percentage of these types of words.

Until recently, these tools have not been used to analyze the speech production of criminals and psychopathic individuals. A previous study using human coders found that there are differences in the speech of psychopaths and nonpsychopaths. Experts found that psychopaths more likely will exaggerate the spontaneity of their homicides. They may label a cold-blooded murder as a crime of passion and omit incriminating details of what occurred during the act.[5] Research on speech acoustics indicated that psychopaths do not differentiate in voice emphasis between neutral and emotional words. Other analysis suggested that the speech narratives of these individuals are organized poorly and incoherent.[6] This is surprising because psychopaths are excellent storytellers who successfully con others.

This finding leads to the interesting question of how psychopaths can have such manipulative prowess. In addition to their skilled use of body language, recent research indicated that they are skilled at faking emotional expressions, approaching the skill level of emotionally intelligent individuals, despite being largely devoid of emotion.[7] They are capable of adopting various masks, appearing empathetic and remorseful to the extent that they can talk and cry their way out of parole hearings at a higher rate than their less dangerous counterparts.

Language analysis tools indicate that many aspects of language are not consciously controllable by the speaker. Words that linguists call function words are unconsciously produced by people. These include pronouns, such as "I," "me," and "my"; prepositions like "to" and "from"; and likewise, articles "a" and "the." Words can reveal the inner workings of a person's mind, such as the narcissist's focus on the self. While word patterns easily are measured by computer programs, they are difficult for human coders to determine because people tend to ignore function words and focus on content words (verbs and nouns, such as "kill" and "knife"). Because psychopaths are skilled at manipulating, deceiving, and controlling their self-presentation, a computerized tool examining subtle aspects of their language represents a new avenue to uncover important insights into their behavior and diagnosis.

Two automated text analysis tools—Wmatrix and the Dictionary of Affect and Language—were used by researchers to examine for the first time the crime narratives of a group of psychopathic and nonpsychopathic murderers.[8] The results indicated that when describing their murders, psychopaths more likely would provide information about basic needs, such as food, drink, and money. For example, in the earlier narrative, the offender talked about eating, drinking, and taking drugs the day he committed the murder.

Psychopathic murderers differ in other ways of speaking. Compared with nonpsychopaths, they make fewer references to social needs relating to family and friends. Research indicated that the selfish, instrumental, goal-driven nature of psychopaths and their inability to focus on emotional aspects of an event is discernible by closely examining their language.[9] Psychopaths' language is less emotionally intense. They use more past-tense verbs in their narrative, suggesting a greater psychological and emotional detachment from the incident.

The authors' study was the first step in using automated language analysis to further the understanding of the psychopath's mind-set and to begin developing a program for suggesting an individual's psychopathy. An ongoing study is attempting to examine language differences in noncriminal individuals who have high psychopathic indicators.

Interrogators and Investigators
Considering the nature of psychopathy and the fascinating aspects of the psychopath's language, law enforcement officials should keep certain points in mind when interviewing or interacting with these individuals. During an interview, Ted Bundy once said, "I don't feel guilty for anything. I feel sorry for people who feel guilt."

Psychopaths are incapable of identifying with or caring about the emotional pain that they have caused victims or their families, so any strategy to appeal to the psychopath's conscience probably will be met with failure and frustration. This type of strategy will prove a waste of time. It may irritate psychopathic individuals and cause them to be less inclined to continue to engage with their interviewers.

Interrogators should remain aware of the psychopath's nonverbal skills—body language and facial expressions that create displays of sincerity—used for deceit in the interview room. Psychopaths are master manipulators who have fooled many professionals. To facilitate the identification of an individual as a psychopath, it is important to collect as much language as possible. Interviews with suspected psychopaths should be recorded for analysis.

Social Media
As the number of people online increases, so does the amount of criminally minded individuals using the Web. This includes psychopathic individuals aware that this may be a fruitful environment for victimizing others. Individuals motivated to lie do worse when they are face-to-face with a potential victim. Recent research illustrated that computer-mediated environments, such as text-based chatrooms, enhance the ability of liars to get away with their lies.[10]

Despite the difficulties presented by Internet exchanges, several opportunities exist. The majority of online communication is text based, which means that unlike face-to-face contact, online interactions leave a record of the actual words. For example, the Long Island Serial Killer used a Web site to attract his victims and communicate with them. The language from these interactions gave law enforcement officers an advantage when assessing the motivations and needs of the perpetrator. Words provide a window into the minds of criminals, helping to determine whether they fit any particular personality profile, such as psychopathy.

Conclusion
Considering some of the unique aspects of psychopathic language, it might be possible to detect the psychopath in online environments where information is exclusively text based. To catch a psychopath in this context, law enforcement agencies need to be aware of the subtleties of their deceptive communication styles. Overall, there is a need for further scientific research on the language of psychopaths and training in statement analysis and deception detection techniques.

Endnotes
[1] S. Porter, L. ten Brinke, and K. Wilson, "Crime Profiles and Conditional Release Performance of Psychopathic and Nonpsychopathic Sexual Offenders," *Legal and Criminological Psychology* 14, no. 1 (February 2009): 109-118.
[2] Convicted Killer Paul Bernardo Interview on Elizabeth Bain, released for public viewing June 10, 2008,*http://www.youtube.com/watch?v=V6F4_KIU55I.*
[3] Y. Tausczik and J.W. Pennebaker, "The Psychological Meaning of Words: LIWC and Computerized Text Analysis Methods," *Journal of Language and Social Psychology* 29, no. 1 (2010): 24-54.
[4] Tausczik and Pennebaker.
[5] S. Porter and M. Woodworth, "I'm Sorry I Did It ... But He Started It: A Comparison of the Official and Self-Reported Homicide Descriptions of Psychopaths and Nonpsychopaths," *Law and Human Behavior* 31, no. 1 (2007): 91-107.
[6] C.A. Brinkley, J.P. Newman, T.J. Harpur, and M.M. Johnson, "Cohesion in Texts Produced by Psychopathic and Nonpsychopathic Criminal Inmates," *Personality and Individual Differences* 26 (1999): 873-885.

[7] S. Porter, L. ten Brinke, A. Baker, and B. Wallace, "Would I Lie to You? 'Leakage' in Deceptive Facial Expressions Relates to Psychopathy and Emotional Intelligence," *Personality and Individual Differences* 51, no. 2 (2011):133-137.

[8] J. Hancock, M.T. Woodworth, and S. Porter, "Hungry Like the Wolf: A Word Pattern Analysis of the Language of Psychopaths," *Legal and Criminological Psychology,* http://onlinelibrary.wiley.com/doi/10.1111/j.2044-8333.2011.02025.x/full (accessed 5/10/12).

[9] M.T. Woodworth and S. Porter, "In Cold Blood: Characteristics of Criminal Homicides as a Function of Psychopathy, *Journal of Abnormal Psychology* 111, no. 3 (2002): 436-445.

[10] J.T. Hancock, M.T. Woodworth, and S. Goorha, "See No Evil: The Effect of Communication Medium and Motivation on Deception Detection," *Group Decision and Negotiation* 19 (2010): 327-343.

About the Authors

Dr. Woodworth is a registered psychologist and an associate professor at the University of British Columbia, Okanagan.

Dr. Hancock is an associate professor at Cornell University in Ithaca, New York.

Dr. Porter is a professor of psychology and the founding director of the Centre for the Advancement of Psychological Science and Law (CAPSL) at the University of British Columbia, Okanangan.

Dr. Hare is a professor of psychology at the University of British Columbia, Vancouver, and a psychopathy researcher.

Dr. Logan, a retired staff sergeant with the Royal Canadian Mounted Police and a psychologist, provides forensic behavioral consultation and training for the law enforcement and criminal justice communities.

Dr. O'Toole has served with the FBI's Behavioral Analysis Unit and is a private forensic behavioral consultant and an instructor at the FBI Academy.

Dr. Smith, a retired special agent with the FBI's Behavioral Science Unit, is a consultant on criminal and corporate psychopathy for intelligence- and security-related government and law enforcement agencies.

Discussion Question

We know that psychopaths can be very skilled at emulating the normal emotions of human beings. With this said, what can you draw from this article that could be used to understand better if the subject you are interviewing is or is not a psychopath?

DOCUMENTING A SUSPECT'S STATE OF MIND
By Park Dietz, M.D., M.P.H., Ph.D.

Reprinted from November 2012
FBI Law Enforcement Bulletin

MANY INVESTIGATORS HAVE INTERVIEWED SUSPECTS who seemed to know exactly what they were doing but learned a year later that the individuals claimed insanity. Or, perhaps, officers have obtained confessions only to discover that the defendants subsequently claimed themselves incapable of voluntarily confessing.

Violent crime and sex crime investigators in the United States typically obtain as many details as possible from suspects about actions committed during the crime. However, these details do not always include relevant information about the defendant's mental state, and such omissions may introduce uncertainties that make mental defenses more likely to arise and succeed. When the suspect has confessed to the act, evidence of the voluntariness and competency of the confession may become critical to preserve its admissibility.

Even when the suspect denies committing the crime or claims amnesia for the time of the act, documentation of the defendant's mental state at the time of commission could prove important in subsequent legal proceedings. To this end, the author offers investigators an interview protocol to assist them in documenting the critical issues regarding a suspect's state of mind at the time of the offense and the confession, thus preparing them for potential battles in the courtroom.[1]

A Useful Tool

The Dietz Mental State Interview (DMSI) helps collect and document evidence regarding the issues that may play an important role in subsequent charging decisions, suppression hearings, trials, and sentencing.

- Voluntariness of confessions
- Competence to confess
- Insanity defenses (e.g., M'Naghten Rule, Model Penal Code, Irresistible Impulse Rule, Durham Rule, and Deific Decree Exception)[2]
- Diminished capacity
- Diminished actuality
- Guilty but mentally ill[3]
- Sentencing

The author developed the DMSI based on over 30 years of experience addressing insanity and other mental state defenses and advising law enforcement on active investigations. The questions are designed to anticipate the legal defenses available in various state jurisdictions, as well as in federal prosecutions.

Administration

Investigators should administer the DMSI immediately after obtaining a confession from a suspect or during the overall interview and preserve this evidence. The author advocates video recording as the most effective means of preservation—which allows all necessary parties to evaluate the evidence and the methods used to obtain it—followed by audio taping.[4] Even if agency procedures do not include recording the initial interview, the author recommends doing so. As the exact words spoken constitute a valuable part of the evidence to be preserved, microphone quality and placement are important determinants of the ultimate evidentiary value of this interview protocol.

Suspects Who Claim Amnesia
As many as 65 percent of defendants referred for psychiatric examination claim amnesia for a crime.[5] Such amnesia claims often arise in crimes involving alcohol or other drug intoxication and in highly emotional crimes. Some offenders feign amnesia.

If suspects claim amnesia but acknowledge that they may have done the crime, they probably will admit to recalling portions of the offense. Thus, investigators should ask all of the DMSI questions, even though suspects may respond to some of them by saying that they do not know or remember. These instances call for additional questions.

- Have there been other times in which you couldn't remember what you'd done? (If so, the investigator should obtain examples and ask about corroborating witnesses.)
- What is the last thing you remember before the crime?
- What is the first thing you remember after the crime?
- What can you remember between those two times?
- If you did this, why do you think you did it?

Suspects Who Deny Commission
When encountering suspects who deny committing the crime, investigators still may find DMSI questions 1 to 3, 15, 23, and 27 to 38 valuable. Further, interviewers should ask other important questions.

- Why do you think whoever did this selected this victim?
- Why do you think the person responsible decided to harm the victim?
- Do you think the individual who did this knew what he was doing?[6]
- Do you think the person responsible knew he was hurting someone?
- Do you think whoever did this knew he was doing something wrong?
- What do you think should happen to the person who did this?

Interpretation
Defense counsel and the prosecutor will evaluate individuals' answers to these questions. If suspects give no evidence of an impaired mental state in their responses, the case probably will not involve a mental defense. If suspects do show evidence of an impaired mental state, both the defense counsel and the prosecutor likely will seek consultation and evaluation from a qualified forensic psychiatrist or psychologist. Importantly, if this interview produces evidence of an impaired mental state, the investigator immediately should ask the prosecutor to obtain a warrant to collect urine, blood, and hair samples for toxicological analysis.

Documentation of the questions asked and the suspects' responses generally will provide attorneys, consulting or examining forensic mental health experts, and, ultimately, the jury and judge with the most immediate and best documented evidence of mental state—as reported by the suspect—that will become available in the case. Investigators do not need to interpret the results of this interview protocol, and they should seek consultation with a qualified forensic psychiatrist or psychologist if they require a professional interpretation before continuing the investigation.

As an important advantage of including these questions in the original interviews by investigators, suspects will answer them before they have had an opportunity to enlist the aid of cellmates, publications, family, friends, or other sources constructing a mental defense or receiving guidance on how to phrase their answers to feign a mental illness. Also, the answers may suggest further avenues of investigation through interviews with those who know the suspect, as well as through important documents and materials (e.g., diaries, journals, writings, and drawings) for specification on search warrants.

For many of these items, the suspects' response should elicit follow-up questions to ensure that the answer is complete, the interviewees provided all willingly offered information, and the investigator clearly understands the suspects' claims. Some possible lines of follow-up questions are suggested (in parentheses), but these do not represent the only relevant ones. Many will flow from the facts of the case, available evidence, and previous answers by the suspects. When faced with answers that contradict known evidence, investigators should delay any challenge until the end of the interview because confrontational questioning, skepticism, or judgmental behavior may jeopardize suspects' willingness to continue the interview.

Dietz Mental State Interview Protocol

1) Do you know where you are? (Where?)

2) Do you know who I am? (Who?)

3) Do you know why I've been talking to you? (Why?)

4) Do you understand that you have just confessed to a crime?

5) Do you understand that your confession will be used against you in court?

6) Did you confess voluntarily?

7) Did anyone threaten you if you didn't confess?

8) Did anyone promise you anything in exchange for your confession?

9) What do you think will happen to you as a result of confessing to the crime?

10) Why did you decide to confess?

11) Do you feel guilty about the crime to which you just confessed? (If so, why?)

12) Did you do the crime on purpose? (If so, why?)

13) What were you trying to accomplish with this crime?

14) When did you decide to do it?

15) What did you think of (victim's name)?

16) What kind of person did you think (victim's name) was when you committed the crime? (Confirm that the suspect recognized the victim as a human.)

17) When you did this, did you think your actions could hurt the victim? (Confirm that the suspect knew the actions were injurious.)

18) When you did the crime, did you know it was wrong? (How did you know this?)

19) When you did the crime, did you know it was against the law? (How did you know this?)

20) Did you expect to get away with it?

21) Did you think you might be caught? (Why did you think that?)

22) What did you do to protect yourself from getting caught?

23) Have there been times you wanted to do something like this but decided against it? (If so, why didn't you do it then? How was this time different?)

24) Would you have done this if a uniformed officer had been standing next to you? (Confirm the individual wouldn't have done it with a police officer nearby.)

25) Did anyone tell you to do this? (Confirm that they do not believe God told them to do it.)

26) When you did the crime, did you know that society would condemn your actions even if they knew everything you know?

27) Did you have any strange or unusual mental experiences around the time of the crime? (If so, what were they? When did this begin?)

28) Have you ever heard or seen things that weren't really there? (If so, has this been when taking drugs? Has this ever happened without drugs? Were you falling asleep or waking up when it happened? What did you see or hear? Has that happened while we've been talking? Did that happen on the day of the crime?)

29) Do you have any ideas or beliefs that other people think are crazy? (If so, what are they? How long have you believed that? Does that affect your actions? How does this affect your actions?)

30) Do people ever have difficulty understanding you? (If so, why do you think this is?)

31) Have you ever been told you had a mental illness? (Who told you this? Have you been treated? Have you been hospitalized? Were you given a diagnosis? Do you think you have a mental illness?)

32) Were you drinking or using any drugs at the time of the crime? (If so, what, how much, and when?)

33) Were you drinking or using any drugs when you were arrested? (If so, what, how much, and when?)

34) Do you have any illnesses? (If so, what?)

35) Were you taking any medications before you were arrested? (If so, what?)

36) Were you taking any medications at the time of the crime? (If so, what?)

37) Have you ever had a seizure or fit? (If so, did you have one the day of the crime?)

38) Have you ever been knocked unconscious? (If so, when? Where were you treated?)

Source: Park Dietz, "Documenting a Suspect's State of Mind," FBI Law Enforcement Bulletin, November 2012, 13-18.

Conclusion

Some persons charged with crime challenge their own confessions or assert an impaired mental state pertaining to commission of the act. Such claims may prove valid or invalid. Justice is served best if the truth prevails, and including the Dietz Mental State Interview when interviewing suspects will increase the odds of clarifying the too often murky issues of mental state.

Endnotes

[1] The DMSI does not serve as a substitute for mental health training or appropriate mental health evaluations, which must be delayed until after a defendant is represented by counsel according to the ethical codes of both psychiatrists and psychologists. American Psychiatric Association, *The Principles of Medical Ethics with Annotations Especially Applicable to Psychiatry* (Arlington, VA: American Psychiatric Association, 2008); and Committee on Ethical Guidelines for Forensic Psychologists, "Speciality Guidelines for Forensic Psychologists," *Law & Human Behavior* 15, no. 6 (1991): 655-665.

[2] R.D. Miller, "Criminal Responsibility," in *Principles and Practice of Forensic Psychiatry,* ed. R. Rosner (New York, NY: Chapman and Hall, 1994): 198-215.

[3] Ibid., 202-205.

[4] S.E. Pitt, E.M. Spiers, P.E. Dietz, and J.A. Dvoskin, "Preserving the Integrity of the Interview: The Value of Videotape," *Journal of Forensic Sciences* 44 (1999): 1287-1291.

5 J.W. Bradford and S.M. Smith, "Amnesia and Homicide: The Padola Case and a Study of Thirty Cases," *Bulletin of the American Academy of Psychiatry and Law* 7 (1979): 219-231.

6 Male examples are used strictly for illustrative purposes.

Discussion Question

The author provides a number of questions that are designed to go to the heart of the matter in connection with the subject's state of mind. Do you think the questions will accomplish their stated goal? Why or why not? Consider the cleverness of the subject when providing your answer.

LOOKING BEHIND THE MASK
IMPLICATIONS FOR INTERVIEWING PSYCHOPATHS

by

Mary Ellen O'Toole, Ph.D.; Matt Logan, Ph.D.; and
Sharon Smith, Ph.D.

Reprinted from July 2012
FBI Law Enforcement Bulletin

GARY LEON RIDGWAY, THE INFAMOUS GREEN RIVER Killer, sat calmly as he casually described how he murdered, sexually violated, and disposed of the bodies of at least 48 women in King County, Washington.[1] He talked about his victims as mere objects, not human beings. He said things, like "I feel bad for the victims," and even cried at times. However, genuine feelings of remorse for his actions and empathy for the pain he caused the victims and their families were absent. Like many serial sexual killers, Ridgway exhibited many of the traits and characteristics of psychopathy that emerged in his words and behaviors during his interviews with law enforcement.

Ridgway had a lot to lose by talking to investigators. So, why did one of America's most prolific serial sexual killers spend nearly 6 months talking about his criminal career that involved egregious and sexually deviant behavior? Because of the strategies investigators employed to look behind the mask into the psychopathic personality, Ridgway was highly motivated to take them inside his criminal mind.

The Interview Experience

There are no materials in criminology textbooks on interviewing an evil person or a monster, terms frequently used to describe a psychopath. These terms have no meaning in the legal or mental health nomenclature. A psychopathic individual is not necessarily evil nor a monster. A psychopath is someone with specific personality traits and characteristics.

Many law enforcement professionals consider themselves skilled interviewers because of their training and the volume of interviews they have conducted throughout their careers. However, when interviewing psychopaths, the dynamics change, and existing skills can prove inadequate. Interviews with these individuals quickly can derail unless investigators understand what to anticipate and how to use the psychopath's own personality traits as tools to elicit information.

Psychopathic Traits

A knowledgeable investigator can identify a multitude of psychopathic traits and characteristics by reviewing crime scene information, file data, prior interviews, mental health assessments, and relevant information provided by associates and family members. When sorting through this documentation, interviewers should look for lifetime patterns of behavior that manifest traits of psychopathy.

Glib and Charming

Psychopaths often exude charm and charisma, making them compelling, likeable, and believable during interviews. They can display a sense of humor and be pleasant to talk with. Their charm allows them to feign concern and emotion, even crying while they profess their innocence. Because it is in their best interest, throughout their lives they have convinced people that they have normal emotions. If they perceive that their charm is not working, it quickly will vanish, being replaced by a more aggressive or abrasive approach. Interviewers are inclined to lecture or scold the psychopath; however, these strategies likely will not work.

Psychopaths often appear at ease during interviews that most people would find stressful or overwhelming. Several explanations exist for their apparent lack of concern, including an absence of social anxiety. They seek or create exciting or risky situations that put them on the edge.

Interviewers often are nervous or anxious. During the first 5 minutes of the interview, when impressions are being formed, engaging in small talk, fidgeting with cell phones or notepads, or showing uncertainty regarding seating arrangements can communicate to psychopaths that interrogators are nervous or unsure of themselves. Psychopathic individuals view this as a weakness.

Stimulation Seeking
Their need for stimulation and proneness to boredom means psychopaths often become disinterested, distracted, or disconnected during interviews. A single investigator may not provide sufficient stimulation and challenge. Consequently, the dynamics need to change to keep the psychopathic offender engaged. This may involve using multiple interviewers, switching topics, or varying approaches. The interviewer's strategies may include using photographs or writings to supplement a question-and-answer format, letting suspects write down ideas and comments for

discussion, or having the psychopath act as a teacher giving a course about criminal behavior and providing opinions about the crime.

Narcissistic

A psychopath's inherent narcissism, selfishness, and grandiosity comprise foundations for theme building. Premises used in past successful interviews of psychopathic serial killers focused on praising their intelligence, cleverness, and skill in evading capture as compared with other serial killers.[2] Because of psychopaths' inflated sense of self worth and importance, interviewers should anticipate that these suspects will feel superior to them. Psychopathic individuals' arrogance makes them appear pseudointellectual or reflects a duping delight— enjoyment at playing a cat-and-mouse game with the interrogator.

Stressing the seriousness of the crime is a waste of time with psychopathic suspects. They do not care. As distasteful as it might be, investigators should be prepared to stroke psychopaths' egos and provide them with a platform to brag and pontificate. It is better to emphasize their unique ability to devise such an impressive crime, execute and narrate the act, evade capture, trump investigators, and generate media interest about themselves.

Irresponsible

The possibility that psychopaths' actions may result in them going to jail has little impact on their decisions. Therefore, pointing out the consequences of their behavior will not work. Their unrealistic goal setting causes many psychopathic offenders to believe they will escape charges, win an appeal, have a new trial, or receive an acquittal. Unable to accept blame, these individuals quickly minimize their involvement in anything that negatively reflects on them. They usually avoid responsibility for their actions and frequently deny that real problems exist. Investigators can connect with psychopathic offenders by minimizing the problem or the extent of the damage. This facilitates the suspect's disclosure of details about the offense.

Pathologically Deceptive and Manipulative
Most psychopaths are pathological liars who will lie for the sake of getting away with it. They will lie about anything, even issues that are insignificant to the crime or investigation. Lying is not a concern for them, and they do not feel anxious or guilty about doing it. Challenging a psychopathic individual's statements will be counterproductive, especially if done too early in the interview. Investigators should keep psychopaths talking so their contradictions and inconsistencies mount. Their arrogance and impulsive nature result in bragging, preaching, trying to make an impression, or just showing off. This is when they slip and provide important information about themselves and their crimes.

Interviewers should be prepared for a psychopathic suspect to hijack the interview by bringing up topics that have nothing to do with the crime. This can result in a loss of valuable time. To bring the discussion back on track an interrogator could say "You raise important issues that I had not thought of, but right now I want to get back to discussing the crime."

Predator
Generally, psychopaths are predators who view others around them as prey. Whether the suspect is dressed in a suit or in dirty, ragged street clothes, this mind-set carries over and impacts the interview. This means the psychopathic individual may attempt to invade the interviewer's personal space. These offenders might note and react negatively when interrogators write things down and when they do not. They will watch

the interrogator's behavior for signs of nervousness, anxiety, frustration, and anger and react to those signs. Psychopaths use what they can to their advantage.

While incarcerated in San Quentin State Prison in California, infamous cult leader Charles Manson participated in an on-camera interview with a well-known national news correspondent. Prior to the interview, prison officers set up the room and told Manson where to sit. There were three armed correctional officers present to monitor Manson's behavior. Upon entering the room, Manson immediately walked around the tables to the other side where the reporter stood. He physically leaned into the reporter, touched him on his shoulders, and shook his hand. This display of arrogance, dominance, and invasion of personal space, which took less than 1 minute, caught the reporter completely off guard. When they sat down, in an effort to build rapport, the correspondent tried to talk with Manson about the beautiful California weather. Manson ignored him, but said that he had just come out of solitary confinement. The reporter asked Manson to talk about a routine day there at the prison.

Some interviewers would reprehend Manson on his behavior, order him to the other side of the room, and let him know who is in charge. Invading another's space and trying to take charge are behaviors that a psychopath will exhibit throughout an interview. Investigators should anticipate these actions.

Manson had just come out of solitary confinement, where he likely was bored. Asking what his routine was like would have catapulted Manson back into a state of mind—boredom—inconsistent with a psychopath's need for thrill and excitement. Manson's actions suggested that he needed to feel dominant and in control. In this case, an interviewer could have focused on Manson and let him feel that he decided the topic by asking open-ended questions, such as "What do you want to talk about?" Interrogators needed to minimize personal views and insights; seek Manson's opinion; and ask about his greatness, crimes, and notoriety compared with others. Law enforcement officers should be aware of the psychopath's early onset boredom and be prepared to incorporate strategies to keep the individual stimulated and interested.

Unremorseful and Nonempathetic
Psychopathic offenders are not sensitive to altruistic interview themes, such as empathy for their victims or remorse over their crimes. Their concern is for themselves and the impact the meeting will have on them. Psychopaths blame their victims for what happened and consider the victims' fate irrelevant.

Many psychopaths have the intellect to understand that others experience strong emotions. These individuals have learned to simulate sentiment to get what they want. When pressed to explain in detail their feelings about their victim, the crime, or the damage caused, a psychopath's words, descriptors, and concomitant behaviors will be lacking.

Throughout the interview, interrogators should include detailed questions about the psychopath's emotions, such as "How did you feel when you learned the police were investigating you?" or "What do sadness and regret feel like to you?" Probing with emotional questions likely will rattle and frustrate psychopaths because they cannot explain feelings they do not have or consider important. Often, these questions evoke agitated responses that are helpful to interviewers.

After asking feeling questions, interviewers should pose intellectual ones about the crime scene, victim, or offense, suggesting that mistakes occurred during the crime. The combination of frustration with emotional questions and inferences of a flawed crime will result in irritation because psychopaths' grandiosity in thinking means that they feel they do not make mistakes. This annoyance results in psychopaths making impulsive, uncensored statements that may help investigators.

Rapport Building

Interviewers establish trust and bond with psychopaths by finding common ground. This involves disclosing personal information, including opinions, thoughts, observations, and feelings. Bonding or emotionally connecting with psychopathic individuals does not work because they have a myopic view of a world that revolves solely around them. They do not care about the interviewer's feelings or personal experiences. Interviewers must connect with psychopaths by making them think the interview is about them.

Conclusion

Through their behavior, psychopaths' convince interviewers that they have remorse when they have none and that they feel guilt when they do not. Their glib and charming style causes law enforcement officers to believe the suspects were not involved in the crime. The psychopathic individual's grandiosity and arrogance offends investigators. Their pathological lying frustrates and derails the interviewer's best efforts. However, with the proper preparation, knowledge, and understanding of psychopathy, law enforcement investigators can go behind the mask and see the true psychopathic personality beneath. Using dynamic and subtly changing strategies during interviews can create an environment where psychopaths less likely will predict the next steps and more likely will talk about their offenses and criminal superiority.

Endnotes

[1] King County Sheriff's Office, "Green River Homicides Investigation," *http://www.kingcounty.gov/safety/sheriff/E nforcement/Investigations/GreenRiver/aspx* (accessed January 30, 2012).

[2] U.S. Department of Justice, Federal Bureau of Investigation, *Serial Murder: Multidisciplinary Perspectives for Investigators* (Washington, DC, 2005), *http://www.fbi.gov/stats-services/publications/serial-murder* (accessed January 18, 2012).

Dr. O'Toole has served with the FBI's Behavioral Analysis Unit and is a private forensic behavioral consultant and an instructor at the FBI Academy.

Dr. Logan, a retired staff sergeant with the Royal Canadian Mounted Police and a psychologist, provides forensic behavioral consultation and training for the law enforcement and criminal justice communities.

Dr. Smith, a retired special agent with the FBI's Behavioral Science Unit, is a consultant on criminal and corporate psychopathy for intelligence- and security-related government and law enforcement agencies.

Discussion Question

The author is absolutely correct in that investigators—regardless of the number of interviews undertaken—can see their interviews quickly go south when they do not understand many of the personality traits and characteristics of the psychopath. Quite similarly, an individual who understands psychopaths but has no real experience interviewing criminal suspects risks similar failures.

How do you think the backgrounds of experienced police investigators and behavioral support personnel can be combined for ultimate success?

The Predator:
When the Stalker is a Psychopath

By

By Sharon S. Smith, Ph.D., Mary Ellen O'Toole, Ph.D.,
and Robert D. Hare, Ph.D.

Reprinted from July 2012
FBI Law Enforcement Bulletin

SAMUEL BROWN WAS A TOP EXECUTIVE OF A FORTUNE 500 company.[1] Although he had a net worth of nearly $10 million, he was a family man with simple tastes and eschewed the trappings of power and wealth. Brown was a low-risk victim for violence. He resided with his wife in an affluent neighborhood where violent crime seemed nonexistent.

One morning, as was his custom, Brown dressed, left his home, tossed his briefcase into his car, and started the engine. As he walked to the end of his driveway to retrieve the morning paper, Anthony Lake jumped out of a nearby van and drew his gun. In the ensuing struggle, Lake fired his gun, wounding Brown, then shoved him into the van and drove away. Lake's female accomplice, tasked to drive a second (getaway) car, left the scene at the same time.

Brown died a painful death just days after he was kidnapped. Yet, over the next several weeks, Lake and his accomplice victimized the Brown family with an elaborate extortion scheme. They made numerous phone calls and sent a number of detailed ransom notes to the victim's family and employer, demanding $12 million for his safe release. Nearly 3 months following the abduction, Samuel Brown's decomposed body was found in a shallow grave.

Stalking

This case study examines the implications of psychopathy in crime scene analyses, specifically of stalking, threatening, and attendant assaultive behaviors. The study also illustrates specific crime scene behaviors that suggest an offender with psychopathic personality traits, as well as the implications of these traits for investigators. Psychopaths' need for sensation seeking would be embedded in the design of their crime and emerge as a high-risk behavior.

Psychopaths' stalking behaviors tend to be predatory or instrumental in nature. The victim is viewed more as a possession or target for control, retribution, or revenge, rather than as the object of a pathologically based fantasy, obsession, or infatuation.[2] Further, psychopaths tend to become bored rather quickly and are thought to engage in short-term stalking with financial goals or those related to power and control.

Though most investigators are not qualified to conduct a formal clinical evaluation for the presence of psychopathy, even a few traits and behaviors inferred from the crime scene analysis may prove sufficient to generate a working hypothesis that the perpetrator of the crime is psychopathic. False positives concerning the potential presence of psychopathy during a stalking or threat investigation are unlikely to adversely affect the outcome of the investigation. However, failure to correctly interpret signs of psychopathic traits could significantly and negatively impact the outcome of a case, even to the extent of compromising the well-being of victims.

Victimization
Lake spent a great deal of time, effort, and personal resources while planning his crime. He watched Brown's house for months, recorded his routine, and carefully planned the kidnapping down to the smallest detail. Once he abducted Brown, Lake put him in a coffinlike box he already had constructed. Bound with ropes, blindfolded, and with his mouth covered with tape, Brown was kept in an unventilated room estimated to reach temperatures in excess of 100°F. Brown's only sustenance was water, and his only pain relief for his gunshot wound was over-the-counter medication. Although Lake later insisted that he always intended to release Brown upon receipt of the ransom, his victim died a few days after the abduction.

Analyzing the Crime
The authors have not made a formal clinical diagnosis of Lake. Instead, they discuss specific crime scene and offender behaviors in terms of how they interpret them as characteristics of psychopathy.

Predatory and Instrumental Violence
Evidence from the crime indicated that the offender had surveilled Brown over a period of time to obtain information about his habits, lifestyle, and neighborhood. The victimology did not identify Lake's abduction of Brown as reactive violence—an immediate reaction to some real or perceived threat he might have felt. Instead, the primary mode of violence appeared thoughtful, premeditated, and goal directed, therefore instrumental or predatory. Lake's goal was to kidnap Brown, a high-value target, and extort his

family and company for money. However, during the abduction, Brown was shot in the arm while struggling, a violent subact by Lake that appeared to have elements of both reactive and instrumental violence.

High-Value, High-Risk Target
Selecting Brown as a high-value target offered Lake the possibility of a large financial payoff and media attention. However, executing such an abduction was high-risk for the kidnappers. Their plan was fraught with inherent difficulties in terms of realistically assessing how the victim would react and maintaining him over a period of time while avoiding detection and arrest.

Brown's abduction occurred in daylight in front of his residence, located in an exclusive neighborhood with a low violent crime rate. Lake could not have prepared for all possible variables and scenarios that could interrupt his plan that morning, despite his prior surveillances. By selecting that place and time for the abduction, he put himself in the victim's comfort zone and risked identification or apprehension.

Sensation Seeking and Grandiosity
Completing this crime, obtaining the money, and evading capture and prosecution were unrealistic goals and grandiose in design. Kidnapping a high-value target certainly would trigger a quick and powerful response from the media and the law enforcement community, including the FBI. Lake probably was thrilled with this type of attention. Targeting a lesser known or less important individual would not have generated such a response and, as a result, likely would have been less exciting for him.

No Guilt and Callous Lack of Empathy

Brown lay tied up in a wooden box for several days after his kidnapping, entombed in a sweltering storage area and dying in his own waste of a gunshot wound. At the same time, news reports mentioned that he was a heart patient and relied on regular prescription medication. Brown did not have this medicine while in captivity, and Lake made no effort to obtain it for him. Lake's treatment of the victim showed a significant lack of empathy and demonstrated the extent of the physical and emotional pain inflicted.

During the investigation, Brown's wife made several emotional appeals through the media for her husband's safe release. Despite these appeals and Brown's death just days after his abduction, Lake continued the extortion for weeks. However, the tone and content of his demands changed subtly after Brown's death. He no longer provided current evidence of Brown's well-being, such as having him audiotape the headlines of the daily paper. Nonetheless, Lake continued his demands for money using his deceased victim as a pawn. In his demands, Lake maintained that he would release Brown safely once the money was paid. This callous and deceptive behavior showed little regard for the victim or the impact of the crime on Brown's family or community, which was following the case closely.

Conning and Manipulation

Even after Brown's death, Lake continued to submit directives to law enforcement and the victim's family. The extortion notes he sent contained language that was controlling and devoid of emotion. Like a puppet master, he attempted to manipulate everything from a distance. Lake appeared to take particular pleasure in his efforts to deceive the FBI.

Failure to Accept Responsibility

In the end, Lake was defeated by his own elaborate but unrealistic plan for law enforcement to deliver the ransom money. The authorities set up surveillance on him after a call he made from a pay phone. While arresting Lake, they found incriminating evidence in his car, including Brown's home address and bags for holding the extortion money. Although Lake refused to cooperate with authorities, his female companion eventually led them to Brown's body. Despite his callous treatment of Brown and his family, Lake portrayed himself to the authorities as a normal person driven to desperate measures because of circumstances beyond his control.

Antisocial Behavior

The case study is not a single offense that took place at one point in time. This crime involved stalking, abduction, assault, murder, and extortion, which occurred over an extended period of time. Lake demonstrated an ability to manage and sustain complex, layered criminal behaviors over a period of weeks. These behaviors suggested an offender who was adaptable and criminally versatile and who had a clear disregard for the rules of society and the rights of others.

Implications for Investigators

Analysis of Lake's behavior, paired with information from the crime scene, was enough to imply his psychopathic nature and suggest investigative strategies to move forward. For example, it was unlikely that Lake would respond to emotional appeals made by Brown's family through the media for his safe release. More fruitful appeals would recognize and concede that Lake was in control and imply that meeting his demands was a priority for law enforcement. Concurrently, any direct or implied challenges to or offensive remarks about the offender from law enforcement could have resulted in an escalation of the crime.

Law enforcement officers cannot rely on psychopathic offenders to follow through on reached agreements. They likely will not have an emotional bond with the victim.[3] Therefore, the possibility of harm to the victim will not diminish with time.[4] Such offenders are mission oriented and probably will not abandon their crime, at least in the short run. Any suggestions they make regarding future acts that will be done to continue the crime should be taken seriously.

After apprehending an offender, authorities can devise interview strategies based on psychopathic characteristics. Interviewers can assume that the offender may attempt to manipulate and control the interview with a demeanor of arrogance and superiority. For this reason, selecting the right interviewer is important. The ideal candidate will remain unhindered by the offender's antagonizing nature.

Open-ended questions might encourage offenders to do most of the talking. They likely will brag about the crime, berate the interviewer, and allege incompetence in the police investigation. However, offenders' arrogance and sense of superiority may compel them to inadvertently provide information helpful to the investigation.

Investigators' comments about the fate of victims or the impact of their death on the family likely will not be productive because of psychopathic offenders' callousness and lack of empathy. Focus instead should be placed on complimenting offenders and their superior abilities to manipulate investigators, particularly the FBI, for such a long period of time. The interviewer also should devise strategies that appear to minimize the consequences of offenders' actions.

Conclusion

Psychopathy is a personality disorder defined by a cluster of interpersonal, affective, lifestyle, and antisocial traits and behaviors that pose a serious problem for society. The behavioral repertoire of a psychopath includes charm, manipulation, intimidation, lack of empathy, excessive pride, and violence. Each of these is a tool investigators can use as the occasion demands. As evidenced in the case study, a psychopath can display a callous disregard for the rights of others and a high risk for a variety of predatory and aggressive behaviors. Clearly, these characteristics have strong implications for the strategies used by law enforcement and security professionals when they must deal with stalking, threats, and attacks directed at public figures, like the late Samuel Brown.

Endnotes

[1] This article has been edited from its originally published format. See Mary Ellen O'Toole, Sharon S. Smith, and Robert D. Hare, "Psychopathy and Predatory Stalking of Public Figures," in *Stalking, Threatening, and Attacking Public Figures: A Psychological and Behavioral Analysis*, ed. J. Reid Meloy, Lorraine Sheridan, and Jens Hoffman (New York, NY: Oxford University Press, 2008). To protect the identities of all parties, the authors have employed pseudonyms and removed potentially identifying information while faithfully portraying the important facts of the case.

[2] J. Reid Meloy, *Violence Risk and Threat Assessment* (San Diego, CA: Specialized Training Services, 2000).

[3] J. Reid Meloy, *The Psychopathic Mind: Origins, Dynamics, and Treatment* (Northvale, NJ: Jason Aronson, 1988); Meloy, *Violence Risk and Threat Assessment*; J. Reid Meloy, ed., *The Mark of Cain: Psychoanalytic Insight and the Psychopath* (Hillsdale, NJ: The Analytic Press, 2001).

[4] Meloy, *Violence Risk and Threat Assessment*.

Dr. Smith, a retired special agent with the FBI's Behavioral Science Unit, is a consultant on criminal and corporate psychopathy for intelligence- and security-related government and law enforcement agencies.

Dr. O'Toole has served with the FBI's Behavioral Analysis Unit and is a private forensic behavioral consultant and an instructor at the FBI Academy.

Dr. Hare is a professor emeritus of psychology at the University of British Columbia, Vancouver, and a psychopathy researcher

---

Discussion Question

The authors state at one point that stalkers who are psychopaths often become bored easily and engage in "short-term stalking." However, their analysis of the Brown case indicates that the offender had surveilled the victim over a long period of time. How do you reconcile these seemingly incongruent positions?

CIVIL COMMITMENT OF THE SEXUAL PSYCHOPATH

By

John Robert Cencich, J.S.D.

W HAT SHOULD SOCIETY DO WHEN A SEXUALLY VIOLENT offender has completed his prison sentence? Should they be set loose into the community? This is something that the state of Washington has wrestled with. After having released two violent sex offenders upon completion of their time in the penitentiary, they violently sexually assaulted a number of victims.

A special task force was subsequently created to address the issue, which resulted in new legislation relative to the civil commitment of sexually violent predators. As expected, the new law received wide support, but quite naturally, there were some who view such a notion as unconstitutional. What follows is a U.S. Supreme Court decision in this regard.

Seling v. Yung, 531 U.S. 250 (2001)

Washington State's Community Protection Act of 1990 (Act) authorizes the civil commitment of "sexually violent predators," persons who suffer from a mental abnormality or personality disorder that makes them likely to engage in predatory acts of sexual violence. Respondent Young is confined under the Act at the Special Commitment Center (Center), for which petitioner is the superintendent. Young's challenges to his commitment in state court proved largely unsuccessful. Young then instituted a habeas action under 28 U. S. C. § 2254, seeking release from confinement.

The District Court initially granted the writ, concluding that the Act was unconstitutional. While the superintendent's appeal was pending, this Court decided *Kansas* v. *Hendricks,* 521 U. S. 346, holding that a similar commitment scheme, Kansas' Sexually Violent Predator Act, on its face, met substantive due process requirements, was nonpunitive, and thus did not violate the Double Jeopardy and *Ex Post Facto* Clauses. The Ninth Circuit remanded for reconsideration in light of *Hendricks.* The District Court then denied Young's petition. In particular, the District Court determined that, because the Washington Act is civil, Young's double jeopardy and *ex post facto* claims must fail. The Ninth Circuit reversed that ruling.

The "linchpin" of Young's claims, the court reasoned, was whether the Act was punitive "as applied" to Young. The court did not read *Hendricks* to preclude the possibility that the Act could be punitive as applied. Reasoning that actual confinement conditions could divest a facially valid statute of its civil label upon a showing by the clearest proof that the statutory scheme is punitive in effect, the court remanded the case for the District Court to determine whether the conditions at the Center rendered the Act punitive as applied to Young.

Held: An Act, found to be civil, cannot be deemed punitive "as applied" to a single individual in violation of the Double Jeopardy and *Ex Post Facto* Clauses and provide cause for release. Pp. 260-267.

(a) Respondent cannot obtain release through an "as-applied" challenge to the Act on double jeopardy and *ex post facto* grounds. The Act is strikingly similar to, and, in fact, was the pattern for, the Kansas Act upheld in *Hendricks.* Among other things, the Court there applied the principle that determining the civil or punitive nature of an Act must begin with reference to its text and legislative history. See 521 U. S., at 360-369. Subsequently, the Court expressly disapproved of evaluating an Act's civil nature by reference to its effect on a single individual, holding, instead, that courts must focus on a variety of factors considered in relation to the statute on its face, and that the clearest proof is required to override legislative intent and conclude that an Act denominated civil is punitive in purpose or effect. *Hudson* v. *United States,* 522 U. S. 93, 100.

With this in mind, the Ninth Circuit's "as applied" analysis for double jeopardy and *ex post facto* claims must be rejected as fundamentally flawed. This Court does not deny the seriousness of some of respondent's allegations. Nor does the Court express any view as to how his allegations would bear on a court determining in the first instance whether Washington's confinement scheme is civil. Here, however, the Court evaluates respondent's allegations under the assumption that the Act is civil, as the Washington Supreme Court held and the Ninth Circuit acknowledged. The Court agrees with petitioner that an "as-applied" analysis would prove unworkable. Such an analysis would never conclusively resolve whether a particular scheme is punitive and would thereby prevent a final determination of the scheme's validity under the Double Jeopardy and *Ex Post Facto* Clauses. Confinement is not a fixed event, but extends over time under conditions that are subject to change.

The particular features of confinement may affect how a confinement scheme is evaluated to determine whether it is civil or punitive, but it remains no less true that the query must be answered definitively. A confinement scheme's civil nature cannot be altered based merely on vagaries in the authorizing statute's implementation. The Ninth Circuit's "as-applied" analysis does not comport with precedents in which this Court evaluated the validity of confinement schemes. See, *e. g., Allen* v. *Illinois,* 478 U. S. 364, 373-374. Such cases presented the question whether the Act at issue was punitive, whereas permitting respondent's as-applied challenge would invite an end run around the Washington Supreme Court's decision that the Act is civil when that decision is not before this Court. pp. 260-265.

(b) Today's decision does not mean that respondent and others committed as sexually violent predators have no remedy for the alleged conditions and treatment regime at the Center. The Act gives them the right to adequate care and individualized treatment. It is for the Washington courts to determine whether the Center is operating in accordance with state law and provide a remedy. Those courts also remain competent to adjudicate and remedy challenges to civil confinement schemes arising under the Federal Constitution. Because the

Syllabus
Washington Supreme Court has held that the Act is civil in nature, designed to incapacitate and to treat, due process requires that the conditions and duration of confinement under the Act bear some reasonable relation to the purpose for which persons are committed. *E. g., Foucha* v. *Louisiana,* 504 U.S. 71, 79. Finally, the Court notes that an action under 42 U. S. C. § 1983 is pending against the Center and that the Center operates under an injunction requiring it to take steps to improve confinement conditions. Pp. 265-266.

(c) This case gives the Court no occasion to consider how a confinement scheme's civil nature relates to other constitutional challenges, such as due process, or to consider the extent to which a court may look to actual conditions of confinement and implementation of the statute to determine in the first instance whether a confinement scheme is civil in nature. Whether such a scheme is punitive has been the threshold question for some constitutional challenges. See, *e. g., Allen, supra.* However, the Court has not squarely addressed the relevance of confinement conditions to a first instance determination, and that question need not be resolved here. Pp. 266-267.
192 F.3d 870, reversed and remanded.

O'CONNOR, J., delivered the opinion of the Court, in which REHNQUIST, C. J., and SCALIA, KENNEDY, SOUTER, GINSBURG, and BREYER, JJ., joined. SCALIA, J., filed a concurring opinion, in which SOUTER, J., joined, *post,* p. 267. THOMAS, J., filed an opinion concurring in the judgment, *post,* p. 270. STEVENS, J., filed a dissenting opinion, *post,* p. 274.

JUSTICE O'CONNOR delivered the opinion of the Court. Washington State's Community Protection Act of 1990 authorizes the civil commitment of "sexually violent predators," persons who suffer from a mental abnormality or personality disorder that makes them likely to engage in predatory acts of sexual violence. Wash. Rev. Code § 71.09.010 et seq. (1992). Respondent, Andre Brigham Young, is confined as a sexually violent predator at the Special Commitment Center (Center), for which petitioner is the superintendent. After respondent's challenges to his commitment in state court proved largely unsuccessful, he instituted a habeas action under 28 U. S. C. § 2254, seeking release from confinement. The Washington Supreme Court had already held that the Act is civil, In re Young, 122 Wash. 2d 1, 857 P. 2d 989 (1993) (en bane), and this Court held a similar commitment scheme for sexually violent predators in Kansas to be civil on its face, Kansas v. Hendricks, 521 U. S. 346 (1997).

■■■ı

Washington State's Community Protection Act of 1990 (Act) was a response to citizens' concerns about laws and procedures regarding sexually violent offenders. One of the Act's provisions authorizes civil commitment of such offenders. Wash. Rev. Code § 71.09.010 et seq. (1992 and Supp. 2000). The Act defines a sexually violent predator as someone who has been convicted of, or charged with, a crime of sexual violence and who suffers from a mental abnormality or personality disorder that makes the person likely to engage in predatory acts of sexual violence if not confined in a secure facility. § 71.09.020(1) (Supp. 2000). The statute reaches prisoners, juveniles, persons found incompetent to stand trial, persons found not guilty by reason of insanity, and persons at any time convicted of a sexually violent offense who have committed a recent overt act. § 71.09.030. Generally, when it appears that a person who has committed a sexually violent offense is about to be released from confinement, the prosecuting attorney files a petition alleging that that person is a sexually violent predator. *Ibid.* That filing triggers a process for charging and trying the person as a sexually violent predator, during which he is afforded a panoply of protections including counsel and experts (paid for by the State in cases of indigency), a probable cause hearing, and trial by judge or jury at the individual's option. §§ 71.09.040-71.09.050. At trial, the State bears the burden to prove beyond a reasonable doubt that the person is a sexually violent predator. § 71.09.060(1).

Upon the finding that a person is a sexually violent predator, he is committed for control, care, and treatment to the custody of the department of social and health services. *Ibid.* Once confined, the person has a right to adequate care and individualized treatment. § 71.09.080(2). The person is also entitled to an annual examination of his mental condition. § 71.09.070. If that examination indicates that the individual's condition is so changed that he is not likely to engage in predatory acts of sexual violence, state officials must authorize the person to petition the court for conditional release or discharge. § 71.09.090(1). The person is entitled to a hearing at which the State again bears the burden of proving beyond a reasonable doubt that he is not safe to be at large. *Ibid.* The person may also independently petition the court for release. § 71.09.090(2). At a show cause hearing, if the court finds probable cause to believe that the person is no longer dangerous, a full hearing will be held at which the State again bears the burden of proof. *Ibid.*

The Act also provides a procedure to petition for conditional release to a less restrictive alternative to confinement. § 71.09.090. Before ordering conditional release, the court must find that the person will be treated by a state certified sexual offender treatment provider, that there is a specific course of treatment, that housing exists that will be sufficiently secure to protect the community, and that the person is willing to comply with the treatment and supervision requirements. § 71.09.092. Conditional release is subject to annual review until the person is unconditionally released. §§ 71.09.096, 71.09.098.

Respondent, Andre Brigham Young, was convicted of six rapes over three decades. App. to Pet. for Cert. 33a. Young was scheduled to be released from prison for his most recent conviction in October 1990. One day prior to his scheduled release, the State filed a petition to commit Young as a sexually violent predator. *Id.*, at 32a.

At the commitment hearing, Young's mental health experts testified that there is no mental disorder that makes a person likely to reoffend and that there is no way to predict accurately who will reoffend. The State called an expert who testified, based upon a review of Young's records, that Young suffered from a severe personality disorder not otherwise specified with primarily paranoid and antisocial features, and a severe paraphilia, which would be classified as either paraphilia sexual sadism or paraphilia not otherwise specified (rape). See generally American Psychiatric Association, Diagnostic and Statistical Manual of Mental Disorders 522-523, 530, 532, 634, 645-646, 673 (4th ed. 1994).

In the state expert's opinion, severe paraphilia constituted a mental abnormality under the Act. The State's expert concluded that Young's condition, in combination with the personality disorder, the span of time during which Young committed his crimes, his recidivism, his persistent denial, and his lack of empathy or remorse, made it more likely than not that he would commit further sexually violent acts. The victims of Young's rapes also testified. The jury unanimously concluded that Young was a sexually violent predator.

Young and another individual appealed their commitments in state court, arguing that the Act violated the Double Jeopardy, *Ex Post Facto,* Due Process, and Equal Protection Clauses of the Federal Constitution. In major respects, the Washington Supreme Court held that the Act is constitutional. *In re Young,* 122 Wash. 2d 1, 857 P. 2d 989 (1993) (en banc). To the extent the court concluded that the Act violated due process and equal protection principles, those rulings are reflected in subsequent amendments to the Act. See Part I-A, *supra.*

The Washington court reasoned that the claimants' double jeopardy and *ex post facto* claims hinged on whether the Act is civil or criminal in nature. Following this Court's precedents, the court examined the language of the Act, the legislative history, and the purpose and effect of the statutory scheme. The court found that the legislature clearly intended to create a civil scheme both in the statutory language and legislative history. The court then turned to examine whether the actual impact of the Act is civil or criminal. The Act, the court concluded, is concerned with treating committed persons for a current mental abnormality, and protecting society from the sexually violent acts associated with that abnormality, rather than being concerned with criminal culpability. The court distinguished the goals of incapacitation and treatment from the goal of punishment. The court found that the Washington Act is designed to further legitimate goals of civil confinement and that the claimants had failed to provide proof to the contrary. 122 Wash. 2d, at 18-25, 857 P. 2d, at 996-1000.

The Act spawned several other challenges in state and federal court, two of which bear mention. Richard Turay, committed as a sexually violent predator, filed suit in Federal District Court against Center officials under Rev. Stat. § 1979, 42 U. S. C. § 1983, alleging unconstitutional conditions of confinement and inadequate treatment at the Center. In 1994, a jury concluded that the Center had failed to provide constitutionally adequate mental health treatment. App. 64-68. The court ordered officials at the Center to bring the institution up to constitutional standards, appointing a Special Master to monitor progress at the Center. The Center currently operates under an injunction. *Turay* v. *Seling,* 108 F. Supp. 2d 1148 (WD Wash. 2000). See also Brief for Petitioner 8-9.

Turay also appealed his commitment as a sexually violent predator in state court, claiming, among other things, that the conditions of confinement at the Center rendered the Washington Act punitive "as applied" to him in violation of the Double Jeopardy Clause. The Washington Supreme Court ruled that Turay's commitment was valid. *In re Turay,* 139 Wash. 2d 379, 986 P. 2d 790 (1999) (en banc). The court explained that in *Young,* it had concluded that the Act is civil. 139 Wash. 2d, at 415, 986 P. 2d, at 809. The court also noted that this Court had recently held Kansas' Sexually Violent Predator Act, nearly identical to Washington's Act, to be civil on its face. *Ibid.* The Washington Supreme Court rejected Turay's theory of double jeopardy, reasoning that the double jeopardy claim must be resolved by asking whether the Act itself is civil. *Id.,* at 416-417, 986 P. 2d, at 810 (citing *Hudson* v. *United States,* 522 U.S. 93 (1997)).

The court concluded that Turay's proper remedy for constitutional violations in conditions of confinement at the Center was his § 1983 action for damages and injunctive relief. 139 Wash. 2d, at 420, 986 P. 2d, at 812.

That brings us to the action before this Court. In 1994, after unsuccessful challenges to his confinement in state court, Young filed a habeas action under 28 U. S. C. § 2254 against the superintendent of the Center. Young contended that the Act was unconstitutional and that his confinement was illegal. He sought immediate release. The District Court granted the writ, concluding that the Act violated substantive due process, that the Act was criminal rather than civil, and that it violated the double jeopardy and *ex post facto* guarantees of the Constitution. *Young* v. *Weston,* *898* F. Supp. 744 (WD Wash. 1995).

The superintendent appealed. While the appeal was pending, this Court decided *Kansas* v. *Hendricks,* 521 U. S. 346 (1997), which held that Kansas' Sexually Violent Predator Act, on its face, met substantive due process requirements, was nonpunitive, and thus did not violate the Double Jeopardy and *Ex Post Facto* Clauses. The Ninth Circuit Court of Appeals remanded Young's case to the District Court for reconsideration in light of *Hendricks.* 122 F.3d 38 (1997).

On remand, the District Court denied Young's petition. Young appealed and the Ninth Circuit reversed and remanded in part and affirmed in part. 192 F.3d 870 (1999). The Ninth Circuit affirmed the District Court's ruling that Young's confinement did not violate the substantive due process requirement that the State prove mental illness and dangerousness to justify confinement. *Id.,* at 876.

The Court of Appeals also left undisturbed the District Court's conclusion that the Act meets procedural due process and equal protection guarantees, and the District Court's rejection of Young's challenges to his commitment proceedings. *Id.,* at 876-877. Young did not seek a petition for a writ of certiorari to the Ninth Circuit for its decision affirming the District Court in these respects, and accordingly, those issues are not before this Court.

The Ninth Circuit reversed the District Court's determination that because the Washington Act is civil, Young's double jeopardy and *ex post facto* claims must fail. The "linchpin" of Young's claims, the court reasoned, was whether the Act was punitive "as applied" to Young. *Id.,* at 873. The court did not read this Court's decision in *Hendricks* to preclude the possibility that the Act could be punitive as applied. The court reasoned that actual conditions of confinement could divest a facially valid statute of its civil label upon a showing by the clearest proof that the statutory scheme is punitive in effect. 192 F. 3d, at 874.

The Court of Appeals reviewed Young's claims that conditions of confinement at the Center were punitive and did not comport with due process. *Id.,* at 875. Young alleged that for seven years, he had been subject to conditions more restrictive than those placed on true civil commitment detainees, and even state prisoners.

The Center, located wholly within the perimeter of a larger Department of Corrections (DOC) facility, relied on the DOC for a host of essential services, including library services, medical care, food, and security. More recently, Young claimed, the role of the DOC had increased to include daily security "walk-throughs." Young contended that the conditions and restrictions at the Center were not reasonably related to a legitimate nonpunitive goal, as residents were abused, confined to their rooms, subjected to random searches of their rooms and units, and placed under excessive security.

Young also contended that conditions at the Center were incompatible with the Act's treatment purpose. The Center had a policy of videotaping therapy sessions and withholding privileges for refusal to submit to treatment. The Center residents were housed in units that, according to the Special Master in the *Turay* litigation, were clearly inappropriate for persons in a mental health treatment program.

The Center still lacked certified sex offender treatment providers. Finally, there was no possibility of release. A court appointed resident advocate and psychologist concluded in his final report that because the Center had not fundamentally changed over so many years, he had come to suspect that the Center was designed and managed to punish and confine individuals for life without any hope of release to a less restrictive setting. 192 F. 3d, at 875. See also Amended Petition for Writ of Habeas Corpus, Supplemental Brief on Remand, and Motion to Alter Judgment 4-5, 8-9, 11-12, 15, 20, 24-26, in No. *C94-480C* (WD Wash.), Record, Doc. Nos. 57, 155, and 167.

The Ninth Circuit concluded that "[b]y alleging that [the Washington Act] is punitive as applied, Young alleged facts which, if proved, would entitle him to relief." 192 F. 3d, at 875. The court remanded the case to the District Court for a hearing to determine whether the conditions at the Center rendered the Act punitive as applied to Young. *Id.,* at 876.

This Court granted the petition for a writ of certiorari, 529 U. S. 1017 (2000), to resolve the conflict between the Ninth Circuit Court of Appeals and the Washington Supreme Court. Compare 192 F.3d 870 (1999), with *In re Turay*, 139 Wash. 2d 379, 986 P. 2d 790 (1999).

As the Washington Supreme Court held and the Ninth Circuit acknowledged, we proceed on the understanding that the Washington Act is civil in nature. The Washington Act is strikingly similar to a commitment scheme we reviewed four Terms ago in *Kansas* v. *Hendricks*, 521 U. S. 346 (1997). In fact, Kansas patterned its Act after Washington's. See *In re Hendricks*, 259 Kan. 246, 249, 912 P. 2d 129, 131 (1996). In *Hendricks*, we explained that the question whether an Act is civil or punitive in nature is initially one of statutory construction. 521 U. S., at 361 (citing *Allen* v. *Illinois, 478* U. S. 364, 368 (1986)).

A court must ascertain whether the legislature intended the statute to establish civil proceedings. A court will reject the legislature's manifest intent only where a party challenging the Act provides the clearest proof that the statutory scheme is so punitive in either purpose or effect as to negate the State's intention. 521 U. S., at 361 (citing *United States* v. *Ward,* 448 U.S. 242, 248-249 (1980)). We concluded that the confined individual in that case had failed to satisfy his burden with respect to the Kansas Act. We noted several factors: The Act did not implicate retribution or deterrence; prior criminal convictions were used as evidence in the commitment proceedings, but were not a prerequisite to confinement; the Act required no finding of scienter to commit a person; the Act was not intended to function as a deterrent; and although the procedural safeguards were similar to those in the criminal context, they did not alter the character of the scheme. 521 U. S., at 361-365.

We also examined the conditions of confinement provided by the Act. *Id.,* at 363-364. The Court was aware that sexually violent predators in Kansas were to be held in a segregated unit within the prison system. *Id.,* at 368. We explained that the Act called for confinement in a secure facility because the persons confined were dangerous to the community. *Id.,* at 363. We noted, however, that conditions within the unit were essentially the same as conditions for other involuntarily committed persons in mental hospitals. *Ibid.* Moreover, confinement under the Act was not necessarily indefinite in duration. *Id.,* at 364. Finally, we observed that in addition to protecting the public, the Act also provided treatment for sexually violent predators. *Id.,* at 365-368.

We acknowledged that not all mental conditions were treatable. For those individuals with untreatable conditions, however, we explained that there was no federal constitutional bar to their civil confinement, because the State had an interest in protecting the public from dangerous individuals with treatable as well as untreatable conditions. *Id.,* at 366. Our conclusion that the Kansas Act was "nonpunitive thus remove[d] an essential prerequisite for both Hendricks' double jeopardy and *ex post facto* claims." *Id.,* at 369.

Since deciding *Hendricks,* this Court has reaffirmed the principle that determining the civil or punitive nature of an Act must begin with reference to its text and legislative history. *Hudson* v. *United States,* 522 U.S. 93 (1997).

In *Hudson,* which involved a double jeopardy challenge to monetary penalties and occupational debarment, this Court expressly disapproved of evaluating the civil nature of an Act by reference to the effect that Act has on a single individual. Instead, courts must evaluate the question by reference to a variety of factors "'considered in relation to the statute on its face'"; the clearest proof is required to override legislative intent and conclude that an Act denominated civil is punitive in purpose or effect. *Id.,* at 100 (quoting *Kennedy* With this in mind, we turn to the Court of Appeals' determination that respondent could raise an "as-applied" challenge to the Act on double jeopardy and *ex post facto* grounds and seek release from confinement. Respondent essentially claims that the conditions of his confinement at the Center are too restrictive, that the conditions are incompatible with treatment, and that the system is designed to result in indefinite confinement. Respondent's claims are in many respects like the claims presented to the Court in *Hendricks,* where we concluded that the conditions of confinement were largely explained by the State's goal to incapacitate, not to punish. 521 U. S., at 362-368.

Nevertheless, we do not deny that some of respondent's allegations are serious. Nor do we express any view as to how his allegations would bear on a court determining in the first instance whether Washington's confinement scheme is civil. Here, we evaluate respondent's allegations as presented in a double jeopardy and *ex post facto* challenge under the assumption that the Act is civil.

We hold that respondent cannot obtain release through an "as-applied" challenge to the Washington Act on double jeopardy and *ex post facto* grounds. We agree with petitioner that an "as-applied" analysis would prove unworkable. Such an analysis would never conclusively resolve whether a particular scheme is punitive and would thereby prevent a final determination of the scheme's validity under the Double Jeopardy and *Ex Post Facto* Clauses. Brief for Petitioner 30; Reply Brief for Petitioner 9. Unlike a fine, confinement is not a fixed event. As petitioner notes, it extends over time under conditions that are subject to change. The particular features of confinement may affect how a confinement scheme is evaluated to determine whether it is civil rather than punitive, but it remains no less true that the query must be answered definitively. The civil nature of a confinement scheme cannot be altered based merely on vagaries in the implementation of the authorizing statute.

Respondent contends that the Ninth Circuit's "as-applied" analysis comports with this Court's precedents. He points out that this Court has considered conditions of confinement in evaluating the validity of confinement schemes in the past. Brief for Respondent 11-16, 29 (citing *Hendricks, supra,* at *363; Reno* v. *Flores,* 507 U. S. 292, 301-302 (1993); *United States* v. *Salerno,* 481 U. S. 739, 747-748 (1987); *Allen* v. *Illinois, supra,* at 373-374; *Schall* v. *Martin,* 467 U. S. 253, 269273 (1984)).

All of those cases, however, presented the question whether the Act at issue was punitive. Permitting respondent's as-applied challenge would invite an end run around the Washington Supreme Court's decision that the Act is civil in circumstances where a direct attack on that decision is not before this Court.

JUSTICE THOMAS, concurring in the judgment, takes issue with our view that the question before the Court concerns an as-applied challenge to a civil Act. He first contends that respondent's challenge is not a true "as-applied" challenge because respondent does not claim that the statute "'by its own terms' is unconstitutional as applied ... but rather that the statute is not being applied according to its terms at all."*Post,* at 271. We respectfully disagree. The Act requires "adequate care and individualized treatment," Wash. Rev. Code §

71.09.080(2) (Supp. 2000), but the Act is silent with respect to the confinement conditions required at the Center, and that is the source of many of respondent's complaints, see *supra,* at 259-260.

JUSTICE THOMAS next contends that we incorrectly assume that the Act is civil, instead of viewing the Act as *'"otherwise ... civil,'* or civil 'on its face.'" *Post,* at 270 (emphasis added by THOMAS, J.). However the Washington Act is described, our analysis in this case turns on the prior finding by the Washington Supreme Court that the Act is civil, and this Court's decision in *Hendricks* that a nearly identical Act was civil. Petitioner could not have claimed that the Washington Act is "otherwise" or "facially" civil without relying on those prior decisions.

In dissent, JUSTICE STEVENS argues that we "incorrectly assumed" that the Act is "necessarily civil," *post,* at 275, but the case has reached this Court under that very assumption. The Court of Appeals recognized that the Act is civil, and treated respondent's claim as an individual, "as-applied" challenge to the Act. The Court of Appeals then remanded the case to the District Court for an evidentiary hearing to determine respondent's conditions of confinement. Contrary to the dissent's characterization of the case, the Court of Appeals did not purport to undermine the validity of the Washington Act as a civil confinement scheme. The court did not conclude that respondent's allegations, if substantiated, would be sufficient to refute the Washington Supreme Court's conclusion that the Act is civil, and to require the release of all those confined under its authority. The Ninth Circuit addressed only respondent's individual case, and we do not decide claims that are not presented by the decision below. *Matsushita Elec. Industrial Co.* v. *Epstein, 516* U. S. 367, 379 (1996).

We reject the Ninth Circuit's "as applied" analysis for double jeopardy and *ex post facto* claims as fundamentally flawed.

Our decision today does not mean that respondent and others committed as sexually violent predators have no remedy for the alleged conditions and treatment regime at the Center. The text of the Washington Act states that those confined under its authority have the right to adequate care and individualized treatment. Wash. Rev. Code § 71.09.080(2) (Supp. 2000); Brief for Petitioner 14. As petitioner acknowledges, if the Center fails to fulfill its statutory duty, those confined may have a state law cause of action. Tr. of Oral Arg. 6, 10-11, 52. It is for the Washington courts to determine whether the Center is operating in accordance with state law and provide a remedy.

State courts, in addition to federal courts, remain competent to adjudicate and remedy challenges to civil confinement schemes arising under the Federal Constitution. As noted above, the Washington Supreme Court has already held that the Washington Act is civil in nature, designed to incapacitate and to treat.

In re Young, 122 Wash. 2d, at 18-25, 857 P. 2d, at 996-1000. Accordingly, due process requires that the conditions and duration of confinement under the Act bear some reasonable relation to the purpose for which persons are committed. *Foucha* v. *Louisiana,* 504 U.S. 71, 79*(1992); Youngberg* v. *Romeo,* 457 U.S. 307, 324 (1982); *Jackson* v. *Indiana,* 406 U.S. 715, 738 (1972).

Finally, we note that a § 1983 action against the Center is pending in the Western District of Washington. See *supra,* at 257. The Center operates under an injunction that implements a plan for training and hiring competent sex offender therapists; to improve relations between residents and treatment providers; to implement a treatment program for residents containing elements required by prevailing professional standards; to develop individual treatment programs; and to provide a psychologist or psychiatrist expert in the diagnosis and treatment of sex offenders to supervise the staff. App. 67. A Special Master has assisted in bringing the Center into compliance with the injunction. In its most recent published opinion on the matter, the District Court noted some progress at the Center in meeting the requirements of the injunction. *Turay* v. *Seling,* 108 F. Supp. 2d, at 1154-1155.

This case gives us no occasion to consider how the civil nature of a confinement scheme relates to other constitutional challenges, such as due process, or to consider the extent to which a court may look to actual conditions of confinement and implementation of the statute to determine in the first instance whether a confinement scheme is civil in nature. JUSTICE SCALIA, concurring, contends that conditions of confinement are irrelevant to determining whether an Act is civil unless state courts have interpreted the Act as permitting those conditions. By contrast, JUSTICE STEVENS would consider conditions of confinement at any time in order to gain "full knowledge of the effects of the statute." *Post,* at 277.

Whether a confinement scheme is punitive has been the threshold question for some constitutional challenges. See, *e. g., Kansas* v. *Hendricks,* 521 U. S. 346 (1997) (double jeopardy and *ex post facto); United States* v. *Salerno,* 481 U. S. 739 (1987) (due process); *Allen* v. *Illinois,* 478 U. S. 364 (1986) (Fifth Amendment privilege against self-incrimination).

Whatever these cases may suggest about the relevance of conditions of confinement, they do not endorse the approach of the dissent, which would render the inquiry into the "effects of the statute," *post*, at 277, completely open ended. In one case, the Court refused to consider alleged confinement conditions because the parties had entered into a consent decree to improve conditions. *Flores*, 507 U. S., at 301.

The Court presumed that conditions were in compliance with the requirements of the consent decree. *Ibid.* In another case, the Court found that anecdotal case histories and a statistical study were insufficient to render a regulatory confinement scheme punitive. *Martin*, 467 U. S., at 272. In such cases, we have decided whether a confinement scheme is punitive notwithstanding the inherent difficulty in ascertaining current conditions and predicting future events.

We have not squarely addressed the relevance of conditions of confinement to a first instance determination, and that question need not be resolved here. An Act, found to be civil, cannot be deemed punitive "as applied" to a single individual in violation of the Double Jeopardy and *Ex Post Facto* Clauses and provide cause for release.

The judgment of the United States Court of Appeals for the Ninth Circuit is therefore reversed, and the case is remanded for further proceedings consistent with this opinion.

It is so ordered.

Discussion Question

After having read the Supreme Court decision, and considering any other sources, discuss whether you support the notion of civil commitments for sexual predators. Is this a slippery slope? Could the next step be civil commitments of political dissidents or white collar criminals?

THE MENTAL STATE OF WAR CRIMINALS AND THOSE WHO COMMIT CRIMES AGAINST HUMANITY

By

John Robert Cencich, J.S.D.

DURING MY PROFESSIONAL CAREER, I HAVE INVESTIGATED some of the worst criminals known to mankind. These men have tortured, sexually assaulted, maimed, and murdered women, children, the elderly, and the infirm. In 2013 I wrote a book, *The Devil's Garden: A War Crimes Investigator's Story*, which provides an inside look at the world of war criminals and others who commit crimes against all of humanity.

When I first arrived at The Hague in the Netherlands, I entered a venue like no other. What I am providing here are some limited excerpts from the *Devil's Garden*, which will hopefully serve to provide a snapshot of the types of criminals my colleagues I dealt with on a daily basis.

I begin by describing the case of the Convicts Battalion that I worked during my first two years with the United Nations:

Other battalion members came right off a page of E. M. Nathanson's *The Dirty Dozen*: they were convicts who had been released from prison simply for the fight. And as I came to know more about the case, it became clear to me that these prisoners were far more deadly than their cinematic counterparts. They enjoyed what they were doing, and the murders of innocent civilians meant nothing to them. They were cold-blooded murderers who, I later learned through interviews and interrogations, often fantasized about raping, torturing, and killing their victims, even before committing these acts.

I often wondered what caused these men to do what they did. Was it psychopathy, hatred, or a twisted sense of ultranationalism? Through the next four years, I came to the conclusion that it was most likely several combinations of these and other causes. For members of the KB, it was all of the above.

More than five years later [after the war crimes], on a blistering hot summer day, I walked into what had once been the primary schoolhouse in the village of Sovići. The windows were all gone, part of the roof was missing, and it looked as though it was all that remained after an apocalyptic war. The survivors provided me with similar characterizations.

Surrounded by a personal protection team from the NATO-led Stabilization Force (SFOR), including Ukrainian soldiers who once were commandos with a former Soviet Union Spetsnaz unit, I began to direct the processing of various crime scenes. As the mission leader, I was responsible for collecting relevant evidence that eventually would be used in court.

As I stood there at the *locus delecti*, I knew I needed to gain a complete understanding of the events that had taken place on that very spot. I needed to sift carefully through the physical evidence, including the actions of the perpetrators, but I also needed to see things from the perspective of the victims. My training in equivocal death and violent crime analysis would definitely come in handy. In many instances, the detailed analyses of the offenders' behavior served to prove the motive for the crime—that is, the discriminatory intent necessary to elevate a murder or series of murders to the next step: crimes against humanity. The same held true for torture and rape as part of a pattern of evidence that demonstrated an overall scheme of persecution.

The OPORD (Operational Order) had been given. The mission: to interrogate a killer code-named "Glock-1" somewhere in Eastern Europe:

On a bitterly cold day I arrived at the prison to conduct the interrogation of the killer, code-named "Glock-1." The prison was located in a dirty, industrial area, and its inmates reputedly faced some of the worst living conditions in any of the former communist countries. Even the prison's psychiatric department was cited as being terrible. Official statistics indicated that the prison also had the highest number of recorded cases of violence among prisoners. I definitely didn't want to spend any more time here than necessary.

I was guided through a maze of dark, damp, and foul-smelling hallways by two prison guards whose pallor suggested they had spent as much time in this dungeon as some of their charges. Soon I found myself sitting in an unventilated, airless room, two stories below ground level. The walls of this windowless, concrete pillbox had a dried blood paint job and a floor made of hard-packed, mildewed dirt. This was the interview room.

Reticent at first, Glock-1 looked to be about thirty-five years of age. His head was shaved, and his face was heavily scarred. He'd been shot in the head and lost his right arm during combat. His intense eyes exposed the horror of the many people he had killed, which was intermingled with my own reflection. There was definitely a certain morbidity about him.

My first task as I began the interrogation was the rights advisement, or "caution." Without it, the questioning would have to cease immediately. The killer's eyes followed my every move with great intensity, trying to size me up. Then, without the slightest hint of trepidation, Glock-1waived his rights and agreed to speak.

He laid out the details of his past violent criminal life, which included cases of armed robbery and kidnapping. Conveniently, as war was breaking out in the Balkans, he had decided to leave Germany to see what Yugoslavia could offer him. His connections were already in place.

First, he went to Budapest for a few days and received funds and documents for his cover. Once in the Balkans, he was provided with uniforms and weapons and assigned to a special unit. He was told that his existence was secret and that if anything happened to him, he would be "erased."

Glock-1 then began to lay out the background that I was looking for. He described his special unit as an ATG, but he looked me straight in the face and said they were not fighting terrorists—they themselves were committing the crimes against the Bosnian-Muslims. Glock-1 was now in a deadly league all of its own. The KB was extremely well-armed, he said, and there were other mercenaries in the unit too. He told me that many found their way from other countries by way of *Soldier of Fortune* magazine. There was more than one "Rambo" with a torn shirt, bandanna, and bandolier.

Interrogation is both art and science. The process is a combination of psychology, sociology, and experience on the street. Interrogating Glock-1 was not easy. A lot of preparation in understanding the killer's mind was necessary, and the dark, gloomy prison setting complicated matters. International investigators are required to videotape all suspect interviews—a good practice as long as the camera and recording equipment are not within the suspect's view. Visible cameras often serve as a psychological barrier to the communication process. Suspects are more reluctant to talk and often shut down altogether. In this case, the equipment was staring right at Glock-1, but despite these obstacles, I got what I was after.

Later as the lead investigator for crimes committed throughout Croatia, I worked with an outstanding investigative team that knew how to work with victims of crimes:

Another eyewitness from Škabrnja explained that his father, a seventy-three-year-old stroke victim who needed a wheelchair for mobility, couldn't escape the violence. His mother, loyal to the end, stayed by her husband's side. The witness never again saw his parents alive. He later learned that his father had been shot in the back of the head; he fell from his wheelchair face down on the floor. His mother was found with a bullet hole in the back of her head and another in her chest. To verify this information, Pfundheller and Hardin provided autopsy reports obtained during their field investigations.

I read each of them, and the corroborating evidence was there. The witness's father had indeed been shot in the right ear and cheek. His mother had multiple gunshot blasts to the head and chest.

To facilitate Milošević's objectives, other crimes were committed by fifth columnists in the region. By artifice and treachery, JNA intelligence operatives carried out special black-flag operations. Saboteurs destroyed churches and synagogues, and agent provocateurs staged murder scenes.

These efforts were not intended to throw off criminal investigators, as is usually the case. Instead, they were meant to make the Serb minorities believe that Croatian terrorists—so-called Ustaše forces—had rekindled their World War II–era ethnic hatred for the Serbs. In reality, Serb forces and intelligence agents were carrying out murders of their own people.

It is no wonder that many ethnic Serbs in Croatia were panicking. These perfidious acts laid the groundwork for the persecution of Croats and attacks on their homes, churches, villages, and helpless families. At one home in Marinovići, a hamlet of Bruška, death came knocking at the door.

"Who's there?" a teenage girl asked.
"Krajina Milicija!"

Our witness, barely fifteen at the time, took the words as a joke—until she heard a burst of fire from an automatic weapon. The girl bolted out of the house with a mad killer in pursuit. She ran toward the woods, but before she reached shelter, bullets struck her arm and her hip. She fell to the ground hard, in pain and panting. Her face void of all color, somehow her mother pulled her to safety. Now the tormented teen was working with investigators under the code name "Jump Rope."

"I felt my body flash with heat, and I fell down," Jump Rope told us. "I realized I had been shot. I was having a hard time standing up, and I realized there was something wrong with my arm."

The attack had occurred just four days before Christmas in 1991, and the bloodshed in the town was far from over. Martić's Police slaughtered at least ten more unsuspecting civilians in Marinovići that night, investigators learned. Nine of the victims were members of the Marinović clan, the family for whom the lovely hamlet had been named generations ago.

Crimes in the SAO Western Slavonia
As I walked the streets of Voćin, I reviewed the evidence and read witness statements taken after I'd sent in a new team of investigators, including a police officer from the Norwegian Police Service. I learned how Serb TO forces had taken over the Voćin police station in August 1991, and how JNA soldiers had followed them into the village. Croatian residents were assembled and told that a new Serb government was in power. The total subjugation of the Croatian population of Voćin was in progress, and a pattern of systematic persecution was under way.

The town of Voćin is nestled in an enchanting valley not far from Papuk Mountain in Western Slavonia.

Perhaps the most exciting thing that happens in this community of less than two thousand is the annual pilgrimage to a centuries-old Catholic church in tribute to the Virgin Mary. But Voćin's serene atmosphere changed on August 12, 1991, when local Serbs declared Western Slavonia's autonomy from Croatia, just as they had done farther west in the SAO Krajina. The SAO Western Slavonia was born—and all hell broke loose.

Like storm troopers, Serb forces burst into the homes of Croats and searched them, seizing hunting rifles and other personal weapons. Civilians were vilified, abducted, and taken to detention facilities. The whereabouts of some victims were never ascertained. My experience told me these were not random acts of violence. Categorical criminal calculation was in play.

Team Four's geographic, demographic, and perpetrator-group analyses were coming together. I knew that the investigators' work was precise, and this had helped to identify an area of Croatia that would provide critical evidence of the criminal plan and key political players in the overall conspiracy. This is what led us to Voćin.

Our investigation revealed that in October 1991 paramilitary soldiers entered Voćin in buses bearing Belgrade number plates. After initiating a sustained pattern of persecution against the local Croats, the Serb forces withdrew on December 13, 1991. They had orders to take no prisoners.

What transpired next constituted both a mass murder and a crime against humanity. Cutthroat killers went door-to-door murdering thirty-two people in Voćin and the surrounding villages. Several tons of explosives were detonated, destroying Our Lady of Voćin Church.

The savage conduct of the killers was difficult to understand, but I knew some of them were sadists. Many of the victims had been beaten with chains, tortured, and burned to death. One woman was brutally murdered by several ax blows to the head. In another case, a Croatian couple had their heads cut off and placed in fertilizer bags. The offenders' pleasure in mutilating the bodies was manifested through their deeds.

Fortunately for us, some of the malefactors left critical evidence at the scene—their military leave records.
These records, together with witness statements, inside sources, and a profusion of circumstantial evidence, later would be used to allege, from an investigative and prosecutorial standpoint, that some of the perpetrators were members of a volunteer paramilitary force known as Šešelj's Men.

To corroborate this information, I undertook a secret mission into the region to meet with a potential witness. I believed she had key information about crimes committed in the area, including details that could help us link the criminal enterprise to Serbia. This reluctant witness had good reason to fear for her life. My job was to gain her trust and cooperation.

I could offer her no assurance of any kind. I could only remind her that working with us was the right thing to do. Winning her over was no easy task, but we did it— and this well-placed source had information that was even better than what our intelligence had suggested. She gave us words spoken to her directly by the highest-level leader in the joint criminal enterprise: Slobodan Milošević.

Meanwhile, there were more crimes to investigate. Some were committed by ruthless men who often wore black tactical uniforms and carried Yugoslav- and Russian-made automatic weapons and radio headsets.

Bold and razor-sharp, their very appearance inspired terror. These were Arkan's Tigers, death squads notorious for their extraordinary violence. When necessary, they hid their faces behind black ski masks, but most of the time they didn't bother. They simply murdered any witnesses, including everyday people such as Juliana Pap. Juliana was a fifty-year-old ethnic Hungarian woman living in Erdut, a village and municipality in eastern Croatia, where both the Danube and Sava Rivers flow. Erdut sits right on the border with Serbia, and it was not a safe place for ethnic non-Serbs.

In mid-November 1991 Juliana went to the TO training center in Erdut looking for her husband, Franjo, and her son Mihajlo. She knew where to go. Mihajlo and Franjo had been abducted several days earlier and fettered in chains. But for some unknown reason, her son had been released. He had run home and told his mother what had happened to him and his father. But before long the terrorists returned and seized Mihajlo again, sending him back to the training center.

The multipurpose facility was used for detentions, interrogations, and murder. It had been established originally by Radovan Stojičić, a.k.a. "Badža," a police general from Serbia who had headed the SAJ. A highly trained killer, Stojičić reported both to Milošević and to the head of the DB. Although the SAJ called itself an antiterrorist unit, its members were the terrorists, not the other way around.

Juliana didn't know it was already too late to find her family alive. When her son was taken back to the training center, he and eleven other ethnic minorities, mostly Hungarians, had been taken to a nearby Catholic cemetery and executed. Her husband was among them.

Anguished and desperate, the iron-willed Juliana tried to suppress her fear as she went looking for her loved ones. She found herself face-to-face with both the head of Arkan's military police and the head of Serbian National Security (SNB). I can only surmise the content of their conversation.

"I'm here for my husband and son."
"They're not here."
"Yes, they are! Please release them! They've done nothing wrong."

We don't know the exact words of her plea, but we do know that she paid for her persistence with her life. From the very moment she pleaded for the release of her family members, she didn't have a prayer. Juliana, another of her sons, and Mihajlo's fiancee were promptly executed.

On June 3, 1992, the head of Arkan's military police once again ordered SNB forces to murder an ethnic Hungarian who was asking about her missing relatives. A simple-hearted woman, Marija Senasi, fifty-four years old, was related to the Pap family. Like Juliana, she never gave up looking for her loved ones. Under Arkan's orders, gun-wielding SNB forces abducted Marija as she pedaled her bicycle down the road between Erdut and Dalj Planina.

Like Juliana, she'd been asking questions around town—and like Juliana, she paid with her life. Marija was taken to a house that was used as an interrogation center and subsequently murdered.

The despot leading the Tigers was Željko "Arkan" Ražnatović, a man with unbridled power and a murky past. His men were vicious executioners enraptured by suffering and death. Often they killed for sheer pleasure; some sanctimoniously made the sign of the cross after taking an innocent life. The fearless Arkan savored the terror, too.

Even before Juliana Pap and her family members were murdered, Serb forces had been busy in the area. During September 1991 members of the TO and the area militia "arrested" a number of local Croats and took them to a police facility in Dalj, a community just north of Vukovar. Arkan was right behind them. On September 21, 1991, he and about twenty of his bloodthirsty men went to the holding tank. Arkan removed eleven prisoners and summarily executed them.

His thirst for blood unsatisfied, Arkan and his men returned to the same detention center the following month. They removed men from the cell block and fatally shot twenty-eight unarmed captives. Their bodies later were dumped into the Danube River.

Arkan's Tigers and their accomplices were just warming up. In early November, killers from the TO led by Arkan and the militia rounded up more ethnic Hungarian and Croat civilians in Erdut, Dalj Planina, and Erdut Planina. They took their captives to the training center in Erdut and executed twelve of them the following day. A few days later seven non-Serb civilians in the village of Klisa were similarly abducted. Two of the victims who had Serb relatives were released, but the remaining five civilians were not so lucky. They were taken to the TO training center in Erdut to be interrogated.

All five were brutally treated, then killed, and finally buried in a mass grave in the village of Ćelija. About a month later, on December 10, 1991, members of Arkan's Tigers and local militiamen whisked away five non-Serb villagers from their homes in Erdut. They also were taken to the TO training center in Erdut and subsequently murdered.

The holiday spirit meant nothing to these killers. Even on Christmas Day, celebrated by Orthodox Serbs and Catholic Croats on December 25 (which corresponds with January 7 on the Gregorian calendar), Arkan's Tigers, members of the TO, and local militiamen went after seven ethnic Hungarian and Croat civilians in Erdut. The victims' pleas for mercy went unanswered. They were conveyed to the TO training center in Erdut, and on the day after Christmas their blood spilled into the snow.

The New Year brought little respite. Within two months Arkan and his band of killers were back at it again. Their modus operandi was the same. They abducted four non-Serb civilians in Erdut and interrogated them in the TO training center. A bloody execution soon followed.

By now the names "Arkan" and "Tigers" caused civilians to tremble in fear. Even hardened criminals blindly obeyed Arkan's every word, lest they suffer the same fate as the Croats and ethnic minorities who fell victim to his terror. Make no mistake: Arkan wasn't operating alone. Although he had direct connections to Milošević, he took orders and pay from the head of the DB—and the DB had its own band of ruthless killers.

In nearby Grabovac, members of the deadly special operations component of the secret police struck hard and fast. This unit of the Red Berets was staged out of Tito's castle in SAO SBWS. On May 4, 1992, a special operations team came to Grabovac and abducted a number of civilians. The kidnappers sped away with the victims in a van, their destination unknown.

Eventually we learned that the kidnap victims, three men and two women ranging in age from forty-one to fifty-eight, were taken to Tikveš Park, near the border with Serbia. There they were executed and buried in a primary mass grave. A secondary dumping site, in an effort to better hide the bodies, would come later.

Investigators knew Grabovac was a hunting ground under the control of the Red Berets at the time of the murders. But the hunters had turned from wild game to innocent civilians.

Throughout the region, many victims' remains were never recovered. Those that were found and returned to surviving family members can be credited, in large part, to the tireless efforts of Col. Ivan Grujić and Dr. Davor Strinović. The mostly expressionless Grujić worked hard as the head of the Croatian Office of Missing and Detained Persons. I respected him immensely, mostly because he worked just as hard to find Serb victims as he did Croats and other non-Serbs. Grujić and his team literally left no stone unturned. Strinović was the deputy head of the Institute for Forensic Medicine at the University of Zagreb. He and his staff of expert medical pathologists worked to identify victims and determine the cause and manner of death. This helped war crimes investigators prepare cases for the prosecutors who would present them in court. More important, the victims' families would have some closure to the tragedy they endured.

UN war crimes investigators from Team Four also were working aggressively. They had the compassion to interact with survivors and relatives. They also had the guts and the sophisticated know-how to work the dark, tough streets and backwoods roads of the region, as well as the inside sources and war criminals who walked them.

This was all evident on October 28, 1998, when members of Team Four solved the mystery surrounding the whereabouts of the abducted civilians from in and around Erdut. War crimes investigators recovered the remains of twenty-three victims, bearing evidence of gunshot wounds, in an abandoned well in Daljski Atar.

It was an excellent operation. The investigative team worked hard and took their missions seriously. Hours upon hours of old-fashioned police work finally paid off.

Investigators, together with Croatian authorities and medico-legal experts, were able to determine the victims using the dates they had gone missing. The first kidnapping victim lay at the bottom of the narrow well. The twenty-two others were piled on top of one another in the precise chronological order of their abductions.

The work continued. In September 2000 investigators found Juliana Pap, her son Franjo Pap, and her other son's fiancee, Natalija Rakin, in a well in Borovo Selo, near Dalj. The remains of Marija Senasi were found too, in another long-abandoned water well not far from the confluence of the Sava and the Danube, at Dalj Mountain near Erdut.

Discussion Question

What similarities and what differences do you see in relation to investigating mass murderers and spree killers in the United States and in an international setting?

Critical Thinking Exercise

In outline form, identify different criminal behaviors and their sources as discussed in the course thus far. Examples include mental illness, psychopathy, borderline personality disorder, etc.

Determining Competency to Stand Trial

By

John Robert Cencich, J.S.D.

REGARDLESS OF ONE'S MENTAL STATE AT THE TIME OF **the act** that placed the accused in court, the mental capacity or ability to assist in one's defense is required under our constitution. The following case is presented in this regard:

PEOPLE v. FRANCABANDERA
33 N.Y.2d 429 (1974)
The People of the State of New York, Respondent,
v.
Leonard Francabandera, Appellant.
Court of Appeals of the State of New York.
Argued February 14, 1974.
Decided March 28, 1974.
Stephen N. Shapiro, James J. McDonough and Matthew Muraskin for appellant.
William Cahn, District Attorney (Henry P. DeVine of counsel), for respondent.
Chief Judge BREITEL and Judges JASEN, JONES, WACHTLER, RABIN and STEVENS concur.
[33 N.Y.2d 432]
GABRIELLI, J.

The novel question posed in this case is whether defendant, suffering from retrograde amnesia so as to be unable to recall the events surrounding the crimes with which he is charged, is an "incapacitated person" within the meaning of CPL 730.10 (subd. 1) so as to be unfit to stand trial as the result of a mental defect which, he argues, deprives him of the capacity to assist in his own defense; and also whether the ruling that he is fit to stand trial which induced a guilty plea to a reduced charge, renders that plea involuntary thereby denying him due process and equal protection. He further argues that the indictment should be dismissed.

Defendant was indicted for attempted murder, reckless endangerment and possession of a dangerous weapon based on events occurring on June 15, 1971 in North Massapequa, New York. Evidence possessed by the District Attorney, consisting of civilian and police eyewitness descriptions of the event together with photographs, is to the effect that defendant, who appeared intoxicated, went to his car, withdrew a shotgun, and commenced firing at bystanders; he then returned to his car and withdrew a rifle which he fired at police as they arrived on the scene. At this point defendant was standing in a doorway and, in response to police demands to drop his weapon, he fired again this time blowing the windshield out of a police cruiser. The police officers then opened fire and one of the bullets struck defendant in the left eye and exited through his left ear. This ended the affray and, perhaps miraculously, left defendant with partial blindness, partial deafness, and the inability to recall anything which occurred after he was cleaning a gun at home and before he woke up in the hospital. The People concede that this amnesia is genuine.[1]

Defendant moved for a determination whether he was fit to proceed to trial. CPL 730.10 (subd. 1) provides that: "'Incapacitated person' means a defendant who as a result of mental disease or defect lacks capacity to understand the proceedings against him or to assist in his own defense."

Following appropriate examinations the court found that insofar as defendant's general mental state was concerned he was suffering from no mental disease or defect which would hinder him at trial except for the loss of memory. On this precise branch of the case there is no dispute. It was determined that he understood the charges against him and the question was narrowed to the point with which we are concerned, viz., could defendant assist in his defense if he could not recall the events constituting the charges against him? The court concluded that defendant should stand trial, that the District Attorney should supply defense counsel with all the relevant evidence, and that the safeguards set forth in *Wilson v. United States* (391 F.2d 460), noted subsequently herein, should apply.

Upon the determination that he was fit to stand trial defendant decided to plead guilty to reckless endangerment, first degree, in satisfaction of the charges in the indictment. The court indicated to defendant that his sentence on this plea would not exceed four years. Before accepting the plea the court went to great lengths in laying a foundation to support the voluntariness of the plea. Witness' statements, furnished to the defendant, regarding the shootout were read into the record and photographs of the police vehicle allegedly shot up by defendant were introduced. The court's rationale in doing this was first, to furnish defendant with all available facts and, also, to indicate to him the degree and extent of evidence against him to support the charges in the indictment so that defendant, even though he could not remember the event, would be in no doubt that it happened and that he was the culprit. The court then explained to defendant the various rights he was waiving by foregoing a trial and then explained that "you can plead guilty without admitting your guilt in a situation that you are placed in as long as you realize that that's what you are doing, that you are admitting your guilt. You are saying I'm guilty not because I remember it but because the evidence that has been presented to me indicates to me that I am guilty and I don't want to run that risk." Defendant, having had continuing consultations with his attorney and family over an extended period of time, indicated that that was the basis on which he sought to plead whereupon, after several more searching questions by the court, the plea was accepted.

Defendant's arguments on appeal are correlative. His contention that he was unfit to stand trial as a matter of law under CPL 730.10 (subd. 1) leads to his other contention that, because of the order finding him fit, his guilty plea was forced and therefore involuntary.[2] These points, however, are but branches of the central issue, to wit, whether inability to remember the crucial events renders the defendant unfit to assist in his own defense as that incapacity is contemplated under CPL 730.10 (subd. 1) or under the due process or equal protection clauses; or even, perhaps, under the Sixth Amendment.

First, it would be useful to examine the nature of the plea which, in the context in which it was taken in this case, approaches the *nolo contendere* concept operative in the Federal courts. Defendant here could not honestly confess his guilt because of his amnesia, but, nevertheless he found himself in a position, considering the overwhelming evidence against him, where a plea to a lesser charge seemed quite the prudent course.

As stated by Mr. Justice WHITE in *North Carolina v. Alford* (400 U.S. 25, 36): "Implicit in the *nolo contender* cases is a recognition that the Constitution does not bar imposition of a prison sentence upon an accused who is unwilling expressly to admit his guilt but who, faced with grim alternatives, is willing to waive his trial and accept the sentence." There is no doubt but that in this case, as in *Alford* where a guilty plea was also at issue, defendant's plea "represents a voluntary and intelligent choice among the alternative courses of action open * * *. That he would not have pleaded except for the opportunity to limit the possible penalty does not necessarily demonstrate that the plea of guilty was not the product of a free and rational choice, especially where the defendant was represented by competent counsel whose advice was that the plea would be to the defendant's advantage" (400 U. S., at p. 31).

The larger question here is not whether defendant knew what he was doing at the time he changed his plea to guilty (and he clearly knew what he was doing); but whether he was put into the position of having to plead guilty because of a mental condition which would have prevented him from assisting in his own defense at a trial. Although counsel raises formidable arguments in defendant's behalf, we are unwilling to hold that defendant suffered such incapacity as is contemplated under CPL 730.10 (subd. 1) or such actual incapacity as would deprive him of constitutional rights were he to go to trial.

Stripped to its core, defendant's argument is that no person can assist in his own defense, or, no lawyer can properly represent a client, who is unable to furnish facts concerning the event charged against him such as names of witnesses, times, physical and mental condition, etc. Here, argues defendant, there is some evidence that he was intoxicated at the time of the shootout; yet he is unable to develop this so as possibly to use it for purposes of casting reasonable doubt on the intent element of the crimes charged in the indictment as would be permitted under section 15.25 of the Penal Law.[3] And, it is argued, in other cases perfectly good alibi claims would be lost to counsel as they are lost to the defendant were we to rule that amnesia is not an incapacitation. (This assumes, of course, that for some reason or other genuine alibi witnesses would not step forward of their own volition.)

There is absolutely no authority that CPL 730.10 (subd. 1) contemplates any situation other than defendant's mental imbalance at the time of trial. Admittedly, that provision can literally be read to mean that amnesia, a persisting condition, could constitute a present defect which affects the defendant's ability to assist in his own defense. However, we are not prepared to hold that the Legislature had anything in mind in enacting this provision other than the situation where the defendant, because of a current inability to comprehend, or at least a severe impairment to that existing mental state, cannot with a modicum of intelligence assist counsel.

This interpretation is borne out in the Practice Commentary attending CPL 730.10 where the seminal case *Dusky v. United States* (362 U.S. 402) is quoted, thus: "the `test must be whether he has sufficient present ability to consult with his lawyer with a reasonable degree of rational understanding — and whether he has a rational as well as factual understanding of the proceedings against him.'" (Denzer, Practice Commentary, McKinney's Cons. Laws of N. Y., Book 11A, CPL 730.10, p. 332). Defendant here was perfectly rational and sane at the time he would have stood trial had he so opted.

There is a growing body of authority addressed to the question here presented. In no case yet reported has it been held that inability to recall the events charged because of amnesia constitutes mental incapacity to stand trial. (Amnesia: A Case Study In The Limits Of Particular Justice, 71 Yale L. J. 109 [1961-62]; Capacity To Stand Trial: The Amnesic Criminal Defendant, 27 Maryland L. Rev. 182 [1967]; Ann., Amnesia — Criminal Capacity, 46 ALR 3d 544 [1972].) In the only other reported case in New York (*People v. Soto*, 68 Misc.2d 629), Judge ALTIMARI held, in a well considered opinion relying heavily on *Wilson v. United States* (391 F.2d 460, *supra*) that an amnesic defendant was entitled to a fair trial and such could be accorded where (as here) the prosecutor makes full disclosure to counsel and where defendant is able intelligently to discuss his case with counsel. The two most often cited cases on this point are the *Wilson* case (*supra*) and *State v. McClendon* (103 Ariz. 105). (Other cases in point can be culled from the secondary sources above cited.) In *Wilson* a case-by-case approach to the amnesic defendant was advocated so that in each situation the Judge would have to prognosticate on the basis of all the circumstances whether defendant was likely to receive a fair trial; and then, at the conclusion of the trial and before imposition of sentence, the Judge would have to decide whether defendant did, in fact, receive a fair trial — this by the application of certain tests advocated by the court.[4]

The defendant in *McClendon*, like defendant in the instant case, suffered amnesia resulting from a head injury occurring directly in connection with the events constituting the crime for which he was charged. The *McClendon* court also counseled that no hard and fast rules should be formulated in this area, and adopted the view taken by the Pennsylvania Supreme Court in *Commonwealth ex rel. Cummins v. Price* (421 Pa. 396).[5]

When it is considered that the result of an order finding defendant unfit for trial in these circumstances would be outright release, assuming the amnesia is permanent and there is no other mental defect sufficient to warrant commitment under CPL art. 730, it can be more easily understood why all the courts which have passed on this question have refused to allow amnesia to be classified as the sort of mental defect causing incapacity to stand trial. This certainly is a consideration in balancing the public safety against the individual's rights; but we do not wish to be understood as making this our prime consideration since it would not fully meet the constitutional arguments. Rather, we are in accord with the reasoning in *Wilson* which addresses itself to the question whether defendant can conceivably receive a fair trial; and, after trial, whether defendant did in fact receive a fair trial. This allows for essential case-by-case evaluation. Applying those concepts to this case we can see that the court could easily have determined (as indeed it did) that defendant's trial would be fair. The alleged crime was played out in front of an audience and the overwhelming evidence, all of which was available to defendant, pointed to his guilt. From this evidence it could be determined that defendant was probably intoxicated. Had they been willing to risk the consequences, defendant and his counsel might have gone to trial on the question of defendant's inability to form the requisite intent to commit the crimes charged because of intoxication. Coupling the prosecution's evidence on this point with defendant's history of alcoholism, which defendant was perfectly capable of supplying counsel and of course capable, also, of testifying to, would have appeared to be the only course open if the decision to stand trial were made and, indeed, this is argued to us in defendant's brief. It is not explained to us, however, how defendant's lack of memory could actually have crippled his defense in this case in light of the nature of the crime and the evidence possessed by the prosecutor. It cannot be said that the decision to plead guilty to a lesser charge would not have been the most astute decision under these circumstances even had defendant been able to recall the events. There is in this case, then, no indication that defendant was deprived of any of his constitutional rights or that the court was in error in denying defendant's CPL 730.10 (subd. 1) motion.

As a guideline for future cases in which defendant claims inability to stand trial due to amnesia proved to be genuine, we approve of a CPL 730.10 (subd. 1) motion (for lack of a better procedural device and although we have held it does not contemplate retrograde amnesia) whereupon the Judge to whom it is addressed shall determine whether, under all the circumstances and with regard to the nature of the crime and the availability of evidence to the defendant, it is likely he can receive a fair trial. If the decision upon the motion is that defendant is not incapacitated due to the amnesia, then the defendant may choose either to proceed to trial, after which he can move for evaluation of the fairness of the trial (cf. *Wilson v. United States*, 391 F.2d 460, *supra*), or he may opt to plead guilty to the best terms he can get.

There is no reason to remand this case for conformance to the procedures just outlined since the trial court expressly made defendant's trial subject to the *Wilson* tests, which, as clearly indicated in that case, could be applied at the conclusion of trial. Defendant thus had the benefit of knowing the full extent of the available options.

The order should be affirmed.

Order affirmed.

FOOTNOTES

1. One of the most common causes of amnesia is severe head injury (see Amnesia: A Case Study In The Limits of Particular Justice, 71 Yale L. J. 109, 110-111; Tuchler, A Review of the Amnesic States: The Significance of Retrospective Falsification, Journal of Forensic Sciences, vol. 2, No. 3, p. 263; 1 Am. Jur., Proof of Facts, p. 507).

2. The People contend that defendant is not entitled to bring this appeal since the guilty plea serves as a waiver of the right to contest the pretrial order made pursuant to defendant's CPL 730.10 (subd. 1) motion. Where, as here, however, a substantial contention is raised as to the voluntariness of the guilty plea because of that pretrial order, there is no question but that the defendant has standing to appeal (see People v. White, 32 N.Y.2d 393, 399). Issues stemming from a guilty plea which involve the legality of the sentence or the voluntariness of the plea itself are always appealable (People v. Lynn, 28 N.Y.2d 196, 203).

3. Section 15.25 of the Penal Law provides that: "Intoxication is not, as such a defense to a criminal charge; but in any prosecution for an offense, evidence of intoxication of the defendant may be offered by the defendant whenever it is relevant to negative an element of the crime charged."

4. "In making these findings the court should consider the following factors:"(1) The extent to which the amnesia affected the defendant's ability to consult with and assist his lawyer."(2) The extent to which the amnesia affected the defendant's ability to testify in his own behalf."(3) The extent to which the evidence in suit could be extrinsically reconstructed in view of the defendant's amnesia. Such evidence would include evidence relating to the crime itself

as well as any reasonably possible alibi."(4) The extent to which the Government assisted the defendant and his counsel in that reconstruction."(5) The strength of the prosecution's case. Most important here will be whether the Government's case is such as to negate all reasonable hypotheses of innocence. If there is any substantial possibility that the accused could, but for his amnesia, establish an alibi or other defense, it should be presumed that he would have been able to do so."(6) Any other facts and circumstances which would indicate whether or not the defendant had a fair trial." (391 F. 2d, at pp. 463-464).

5. Part of the language of the Cummins case cited with approval in McClendon is as follows: "we are constrained to hold that defendant is not entitled at this time (1) to a discharge from the indictment for murder, or (2) to a stay of proceedings under the aforesaid common law test or under the Mental Health Act. This defendant (we repeat) is able to comprehend his position as one accused of murder, is fully capable of understanding the gravity of the criminal proceedings against him, and is as able to cooperate with his counsel in making a rational defense as is any defendant who alleges that at the time of the crime he was insane or very intoxicated or completely drugged, or a defendant whose mind allegedly went blank or who blacked out or who panicked and contends or testifies that he does not remember anything." (421 Pa., at p. 406, cited in McClendon, 103 Ariz., at p. 108).

Discussion Question

Do you think that we should have rules that require certain degrees of mental competency for individuals who stand accused of crimes?

Critical Thinking Exercise

In outline form, draw up a list of factors that should be considered in making determinations of competency to stand trial. You can use those you have read about as well as include any factors you feel would bring added value to such an assessment.

Coordinating Community Services for Mentally Ill Offenders: Maryland's Community Criminal Justice Treatment Program

By

Catherine Conly

Reprinted from the National Institute of Justice

L OOKING AROUND HIS APARTMENT, 45-YEAR-OLD RAY Carver can hardly believe his good fortune.[1] Not long ago, he was living in abandoned buildings and drinking cheap whiskey. He had survived like that since he was a teenager, traveling up and down the East Coast, periodically being arrested for shoplifting or vagrancy and spending months at a time in jail. In his early twenties, Ray was diagnosed with schizophrenia by a psychiatrist in a District of Columbia jail. Since then, he had taken medication sporadically and had been institutionalized twice for his mental illness. Most of the time, however, he lived on the streets and drank heavily.

When Ray was arrested for shoplifting in Salisbury, Maryland, he reported to the Wicomico County Detention Center's classification officer that he had been taking medication for schizophrenia. The officer referred Ray to the mental health case manager assigned to the jail by the county health department through the Maryland Community Criminal Justice Treatment Program. With that referral, Ray Carver embarked on a journey that would significantly change his life.

Thousands of mentally ill individuals pass through local correctional facilities each year. In 1996, one-quarter of jail inmates reported that they had been treated at some time for a mental or emotional problem.[2] Nearly 89,000 said that they had taken a prescription medication for those types of problems, and more than 51,000 reported that they had been admitted to an overnight mental health program.[3]

The dramatic growth of the population of jailed mentally ill persons has coincided with the policy of deinstitutionalization that resulted in the release of thousands of mentally ill people from psychiatric facilities to the community.[4] Additional factors, including cuts in public assistance, more stringent civil commitment laws, declines in the availability of low-income housing, and limited availability of mental health care in the community, are thought to have exacerbated conditions for the mentally ill and contributed to their increased involvement in the criminal justice system.[5] Many mentally ill offenders are charged with relatively minor offenses (e.g., prostitution, shoplifting, vagrancy),[6] but are not diagnosed or treated while in jail and are released back to their communities with no plan for treatment or aftercare.

Finding humane, constitutional, and effective ways to address the needs of mentally ill individuals is a challenge for local correctional facilities nationwide. Crowded, outdated, and designed to ensure secure confinement, most jails are not optimal treatment settings for the mentally ill.[7] Nonetheless, the nature of jail populations increasingly demands— and numerous court decisions require— that jails respond to the needs of the mentally ill.[8]

Researchers consistently recommend correctional strategies that result in early identification and referral of the jailed mentally ill to the most appropriate treatment setting, preferably in the community.[9] However, only a few jails have achieved this goal.[10] Even in jails where psychiatric services are models for others nationwide, a significant proportion of the mentally ill can go undetected and/or untreated.[11] In addition, many mentally ill individuals are released with no plan for community-based care.[12]

Mentally ill offenders are poorly equipped to serve as advocates for their own welfare. They often face multiple challenges, including homelessness, unemployment, estrangement from family and friends, substance abuse, and other serious health conditions such as HIV/AIDS, tuberculosis, and hepatitis.[13] In turn, community-based providers often find mentally ill offenders challenging to serve because of their "coexisting conditions, noncompliance, criminal records, unkempt appearance, and clinically difficult and challenging presentation."[14] Consequently, mentally ill individuals may cycle repeatedly through the health, mental health, social service, and criminal justice systems, each with its unilateral focus, and never become stabilized because of a lack of coordinated care and treatment. This "system cycling" is discouraging to the mentally ill offender and costly to the network of community-based providers.

Overview of MCCJTP

After years of study and discussion, local corrections officials in Maryland worked with others in local government, with State officials, and with representatives from the private sector to create MCCJTP. In various stages of implementation in 18 of the State's 24 local jurisdictions,[15] MCCJTP brings treatment and criminal justice professionals together to screen mentally ill individuals while they are confined in local jails, prepare treatment and aftercare plans for them, and provide community follow-up after their release. The program also offers services to mentally ill probationers and parolees and provides enhanced services to mentally ill offenders who are homeless and/or have co-occurring substance use disorders.

MCCJTP targets individuals 18 or older who have a serious mental illness (i.e., schizophrenia, major affective disorder, organic mental disorder, or other psychotic disorders), with or without a co-occurring substance use disorder. It is founded on two key principles:

- **The target population requires a continuum of care provided by a variety of service professionals in jail and in the community that is coordinated at both the State and local levels.** In this regard, agency participants include local mental health and substance abuse treatment providers and advocates, local hospital professionals, housing providers, members of local law enforcement, and representatives of key State criminal justice, mental health, and substance abuse agencies.

- **Local communities are in the best position to plan and implement responses to meet the needs of the mentally ill offenders in their jurisdictions.** To that end, each participating jurisdiction has developed a local advisory board to oversee the conduct of needs assessments, coordinate program implementation, monitor service delivery, and expand program options.

MCCJTP's goals are to improve the identification and treatment of mentally ill offenders and increase their chances of successful independent living, thereby preventing their swift return to jail, mental hospitals, homelessness, or hospital emergency rooms. In some locations, MCCJTP also aims to reduce the period of incarceration (through postbooking diversion) and even reduce the likelihood of incarceration altogether (through prebooking diversion).

According to data maintained by the Maryland Department of Health and Mental Hygiene, almost 1,700 mentally ill individuals received services through MCCJTP in 1996 (see "The Mentally Ill in Maryland Jails," page 5). Funding for the 18 programs totals approximately $4 million annually and comes from local, State, and Federal sources. In addition, many agencies contribute administrative time and support services (see "MCCJTP Funding," page 5).[16] The funding supports the provision of case management services in each jurisdiction and other specialized services such as housing to meet the needs of mentally ill offenders.

This Program Focus reviews the history of MCCJTP, describes key program features, and discusses the benefits of and challenges to program operation.

The Roots of the Program
In the early 1990s, an estimated 600 to 700 mentally ill offenders were confined in local correctional facilities throughout Maryland.[17] Because they lacked sufficient numbers of appropriately trained staff to screen and treat the mentally ill, jails were neither sensitive, nor especially safe, places for most mentally ill individuals. In those days, according to several local

corrections officials, the special needs of mentally ill were generally ignored unless such individuals were suicidal or disruptive. The disruptive ones were usually "locked down," but not until staff had spent considerable time in crisis management, trying to subdue them or negotiate with mental health agencies for emergency commitments. Lacking mental health training, correctional officers were frustrated and sometimes insensitive in their handling of mentally ill offenders, which exacerbated an already difficult situation. Adding to the concerns of corrections officials was the high rate of recidivism among mentally ill offenders. One frustrated former warden of a detention facility in southern Maryland, who has since become a strong advocate of MCCJTP, admits having asked publicly about the mentally ill offenders in his jail, "Can't we shoot them up with something and just keep them asleep while they're here?"

In 1991, at the request of the Maryland Correctional Administrators Association, the Governor's Office of Justice Administration (GOJA) formed an interagency State and local task force to help define a strategy for responding to mentally ill offenders in the State. After careful review of available national research and reports on the topic by previous State task forces, the GOJA task force concluded that offenders with serious mental illnesses require a coordinated treatment approach that combines the expertise of criminal justice and treatment professionals.

The Jail Mental Health Program pilot
The State's Mental Hygiene Administration (MHA), part of the Maryland Department of Health and Mental Hygiene, assumed primary responsibility for the design and implementation of a pilot program to aid local detention centers in creating a multidisciplinary response to the jailed mentally ill. In 1993 and 1994, with $50,000 in seed money from MHA, four pilot Jail

Mental Health Programs (predecessors to MCCJTP) were launched in Cecil, Charles, Frederick, and Wicomico counties. The pilots resulted in the creation of a system for providing case management services to mentally ill inmates.

Within a short amount of time, those involved in the Jail Mental Health Program began reporting improved identification of the jailed mentally ill, enhanced communication between mental health and corrections staff, and reduced disruptions associated with mentally ill inmates.

Fourteen additional counties have since developed similar programs to respond to mentally ill offenders. Over time, the focus of the Jail Mental Health Program has expanded to include greater use of community-based services and diversion. In addition, mentally ill probationers and parolees have been added to the client base. The program's title was changed to the Maryland Community Criminal Justice Treatment Program in 1994 to reflect its broader scope.

Key Features of Maryland's Coordinated Approach

Immediately after Ray Carver was referred for a mental health screening, the MCCJTP case manager reviewed his history of mental illness and referred him for medication. She counseled Ray throughout his stay at the detention center, and together they developed a treatment and aftercare plan for him that included taking his medication, participating in treatment for alcoholism, reinstating his Supplemental Security Income benefits, locating housing, and participating in the day program at Go-Getters, Inc., a local psychiatric rehabilitation center and partner agency of MCCJTP.

The case manager discussed Ray's criminal charges with his public defender, the assistant State's attorney, and the district court judge. Ray pled guilty and was sentenced to a year's probation. Several components of the treatment plan, which he signed in the presence of the judge, were included as conditions of Ray's probation.

Because he was homeless before his incarceration and willing to quit drinking and participate in daytime activities at Go-Getters, Inc., Ray qualified for housing assistance through the Shelter Plus Care grant awarded to Maryland's Department of Health and Mental Hygiene by the Federal Department of Housing and Urban Development. Prior to Ray's release, the MCCJTP case manager helped Ray complete an application for Shelter Plus Care housing, and a representative from Hudson Health Services, another partner agency of MCCJTP, located an apartment for Ray in a relatively low-crime area of town, just a few blocks from Go-Getters. The furnishings for Ray's apartment—a sofa, bed, table, and chair—were donated by local church and community organizations and moved to the apartment by two of the detention center's work release inmates.

On the day he was released from jail, Ray's MCCJTP case manager spent the day helping him get settled in his new apartment. Together, they stocked Ray's refrigerator, met with the psychiatrist at the County Health Center, and visited Go-Getters, where Ray was assigned a case manager.

For the first month after Ray's release, the MCCJTP case manager checked in on Ray several times a week. As Ray became more involved in community-based services, the MCCJTP case manager's involvement tapered off. She monitors Ray's progress with his case manager at Go-Getters and other service providers and is on-call in the event of a crisis.

As Ray's experience suggests, MCCJTP incorporates key features listed below and described more fully in the sections that follow:

- Local partnerships to aid mentally ill offenders.

- Support from State government agencies.

- A broad range of case management services for mentally ill offenders who are incarcerated or living in the community.

- Enhanced services for mentally ill offenders who are homeless and/or have co-occurring substance use disorders.

- Diversion strategies.

- Training for criminal justice and treatment professionals involved in the program.

- A commitment to program evaluation.

Local partnerships

Each MCCJTP program is guided by a local advisory board that assesses service needs, monitors program implementation, and investigates ways to expand program services. Although board membership varies across the counties, it generally includes representatives from the local detention center, as well as health and mental health professionals, alcohol and drug abuse treatment providers, public defenders, assistant State's attorneys, judges, parole and probation officers, law enforcement personnel, social service professionals, local hospital staff, housing specialists, mental health advocates, and consumers. Additional members are recruited as particular service needs (e.g., for diversion) are identified.

In most counties the advisory boards divide their time between reviewing specific cases and setting or refining policy. In most jurisdictions local health departments or related agencies coordinate MCCJTP and supervise the mental health staff assigned to the program. Other government agencies and private organizations have signed memorandums of understanding (MOUs) delineating their participation in local advisory boards and their willingness to provide services as appropriate.

These formal agreements are thought to be essential to ensure the smooth execution of local policies. In addition, working together to handle specific cases has reportedly been extremely beneficial to solidifying relationships among participating agencies and organizations. As program participants have been able to solve the needs of specific mentally ill offenders, mutual trust has grown and formal organizational agreements have evolved. Shelley McVicker, assistant State's attorney in Frederick County, recalls, "At first we worked out relationships with others in the [MCCJTP] network on a case-by-case basis. Then we worked on organizational MOUs. The State's involvement has helped us cement the relationships."

In addition, the willingness of community treatment providers to provide honest feedback to the criminal justice system about offenders' compliance has resulted in support from criminal justice professionals for placing mentally ill offenders in the community. According to McVicker, "My office has a good relationship with Way Station [a local psychiatric rehabilitation facility participating in MCCJTP]. They share information honestly about those who stay in treatment and those who don't. When necessary, we are able to work together to define reasonable consequences."

Support from State government
A number of State agencies have made strong commitments to local MCCJTP programs. In 1994, in an effort to better serve mentally ill offenders, MHA expanded its priority population to include MCCJTP participants and gave those individuals the same access to MHA-funded services and housing as persons discharged from MHA inpatient facilities.

Other State agencies, including the Division of Parole and Probation and the Alcohol and Drug Abuse Administration, made formal commitments to ensure the participation of their local representatives in MCCJTP.

MHA's Division of Specific Populations has primary responsibility for supporting MCCJTP, providing nearly $1 million in annual funding for the program. In addition, MHA staff have worked cooperatively with local decisionmakers to prepare grant proposals for other types of Federal, State, and local funding to enhance program services and create opportunities for local MCCJTP participants to receive technical assistance and training from the National Institute of Corrections Jails Division and from the National GAINS Center for People With Co-Occurring Disorders in the Justice System.[18]

MHA staff have also been quick to address issues that cannot be resolved easily at the local level (e.g., regarding inmates who require competency hearings or emergency commitment to State mental hospitals). In addition, MHA staff regularly participate in meetings of local MCCJTP advisory boards and the Maryland Correctional Administrators Association. Along with wardens and other local advisory board members, MHA staff have met on several occasions with county councils to discuss the merits of MCCJTP and seek local funding for program enhancements.

Case Management Services

Each MCCJTP jurisdiction employs at least one case manager who is responsible for screening mentally ill individuals while they are jailed, counseling them while they are detained, helping them develop discharge plans, assisting them in obtaining services in the community, advocating for them with criminal justice officials and community-based service providers, and monitoring their progress following release (even if their criminal charges are dismissed).

MCCJTP case managers also help link mentally ill offenders on intensive probation or parole with community-based services and monitor their progress following release. Although most mentally ill offenders in the program are contacted in detention centers, some are not. For example, parolees from the State prison system may be referred to an MCCJTP case manager by prison or parole officials via MHA, or they may refer themselves following release.

In most jurisdictions, county health departments or equivalent government agencies receive up to $50,000 per year from MHA to hire a full-time MCCJTP case manager who is an experienced mental health professional with an advanced degree in counseling. In some jurisdictions, a portion of the $50,000 is used to increase psychiatric treatment time in jail. Administrative support and supervisory hours are usually contributed by the recipient agency.

According to MHA, the average MCCJTP caseload is 35 clients, but caseload size ranges from 10 to 56 depending on the jurisdiction and the number of clients supervised in the community. In some settings, following a period of close supervision by the MCCJTP case manager, community-based case managers from government or private-sector mental health organizations assume primary responsibility for monitoring released individuals, which reduces the supervisory responsibilities of the MCCJTP case manager.

Though adaptations are necessary to accommodate local needs and service capabilities, each participating jurisdiction adheres to the following general case management protocol:

Identification. Preliminary identification of candidates for program services is made following arrest, after self-referral by the defendant, or as a result of referrals by the arresting officer, the classification officer, jail medical staff, the substance abuse counselor, or other jail personnel.

Screening and needs assessment. The MCCJTP case manager meets with the candidates to conduct an in-jail diagnostic interview and an individual needs assessment. If an individual qualifies for program services, he or she may be referred for medication.

Counseling and discharge planning. While in jail, the mentally ill defendant meets with the case manager for counseling and development of an aftercare plan. A typical plan will include mental health and substance abuse counseling, educational services, recreational activities, employment training, and housing placement. Before the individual is released, the MCCJTP case manager and, in some cases, a residential rehabilitation specialist work to identify suitable housing.

Criminal justice system liaison. The MCCJTP case manager also meets with assistant State's attorneys and defense counsel to advocate for the swift resolution of criminal charges (e.g., through diversion or plea negotiation) and for the return of the MCCJTP client to the community whenever possible. These negotiations usually succeed when criminal charges are relatively minor because the MCCJTP case manager is able to ensure close supervision of the mentally ill offender in the community and the quick, honest reporting of any problems.

Referral and monitoring in the community

For those who agree or are required to participate in community followup, [19] MCCJTP case managers help link clients to specified services, such as psychiatric day treatment, substance abuse treatment, vocational rehabilitation, and educational services. In addition, MCCJTP case managers meet regularly with community-based providers to monitor client progress.

MCCJTP's community-based partners are essential to the implementation of aftercare plans. In some jurisdictions, released individuals are able to participate in day-treatment programs offered by local psychiatric rehabilitation centers. These programs offer an array of work opportunities, skills development classes, substance abuse counseling, and housing assistance. They may also assign a case manager to work with the mentally ill offender in the community. In other locations, a mix of providers offer these services.

Enhanced services

State and local MCCJTP participants have become increasingly aware of the need to address certain sub-populations of mentally ill offenders, including homeless persons and those with co-Shelter Plus Care applicants are eligible to receive the equivalent of the fair market rate for rent and utilities in the jurisdiction where they live, provided their incomes do not exceed the predetermined ceiling for the county of residence, they agree to pay up to one-third of their incomes in rent, and they participate in fulfilling the components of their MCCJTP treatment plans. Shelter Plus Care recipients may live alone or with a roommate. In situations involving families, the spouse and/or children are also eligible for housing as long as the adult receiving the assistance will aid in the care and support of the children and the family's income does not exceed the ceiling for the county.

The MCCJTP case manager and/or other case managers available through community-based service providers are responsible for developing treatment plans, gathering documentation of homelessness, and filing paperwork with the appropriate county and State mental health offices. In some jurisdictions, case managers are also responsible for locating housing. In others, such as Calvert, Frederick, Prince Georges, and occurring substance use disorders. State and Federal grant funds are being used to enhance the response to individuals in these groups.

Homeless mentally ill offenders. In 1995, MHA was awarded a $5.5-million Shelter Plus Care grant by HUD to provide rental assistance for up to 5 years to homeless mentally ill offenders served by MCCJTP.[20] In turn, local service providers participating in MCCJTP have pledged to provide services such as vocational training, substance abuse treatment, and life-skills training to ensure that Shelter Plus Care recipients have access to meaningful daytime activities.

Case managers are responsible for monitoring tenants to ensure their compliance with housing agreements and participation in the daily activities outlined in treatment plans. To assist in this process, each service provider submits monthly documentation of the services clients receive to the MCCJTP case manager.

Program implementation has been remarkably smooth. By all accounts, landlords have responded favorably to the program. They appreciate that it guarantees that rents will be paid and that tenants will be supervised closely. In addition, there has been no community opposition, probably because Shelter Plus Care clients are housed throughout the community in single- or double-occupancy dwellings, and because close supervision by case managers helps to ensure that client problems are addressed swiftly. Bureaucratic issues such as creating tracking forms, training staff, and developing protocols for timely rental payments by State and county government agencies have arisen, but are now mostly resolved.

Other issues have emerged as well. First, rental assistance does not cover the costs of such household necessities as furniture, linens, dishes, and utensils. Although these items are often donated by local charitable organizations, they must be moved to the housing locations. In Wicomico County, detention center inmates on work release help transport furnishings, which has proven a cost-effective way to reduce the burden on the MCCJTP case manager. Second, housing is not always located near public transportation. This is especially true in rural counties where transportation to daytime activities is generally limited. In some locations, community-based participants

According to MHA, 216 individuals and/or families were placed in Maryland's Shelter Plus Care Housing Program in the first 2 years of operation (April 1996 to April 1998). At the end of the period, nearly 90 percent remained in permanent housing. Eleven individuals had been evicted; 7 were rearrested; and 9 left the program.

Mentally ill offenders with co-occurring substance use disorders. In 1996 MHA received nearly $350,000 in Edward Byrne Memorial State and Local Law Enforcement Assistance Program funds from the U.S.

Department of Justice's Bureau of Justice Assistance to hire substance abuse and mental health case managers to aid dually diagnosed offenders in seven MCCJTP jurisdictions.[21] These funds are being used in a variety of ways. For example, Frederick County has hired a case manager who provides treatment planning to mentally ill offenders with co-occurring substance use disorders while they are confined in the Frederick County Adult Detention Center and community followup after they are released. The case manager also coordinates mental health services at the detention center with medical, inmate classification, substance abuse program, and security staff. In Dorchester County, a full-time case manager is involved in treatment of dually diagnosed inmates; Kent County uses its funds for community followup of dually diagnosed clients.

Other counties that do not receive Byrne funding have taken steps to ensure that mental health services are coordinated with their jails' substance abuse treatment providers. Substance abuse treatment professionals in the jails report that, as a result of MCCJTP, mentally ill offenders, who often went undiagnosed or untreated in the past, can now benefit more fully from substance abuse services and are less disruptive in substance abuse treatment settings.

Diversion
In a number of jurisdictions, diversion is included among the MCCJTP's objectives. Hoping to reduce the length of confinement for mentally ill individuals who are arrested for nonviolent offenses, Wicomico County added postbooking diversion to its bank of program services soon after implementing MCCJTP. According to the county's guidelines, diversion candidates must demonstrate a willingness to participate in the program, and community-based services must be available to meet participants' needs. Individuals with

a history of violence or arson are not eligible for the program.

In a typical situation, the MCCJTP case manager works with a diversion candidate to develop a treatment plan. The treatment plan is then discussed with the assistant State's attorney, the public defender, and the judge assigned to the case. When all parties agree that diversion is appropriate, the judge places the case on the "stet" docket, which leaves it open for 1 year. The defendant is then released to the community to complete his or her treatment plan. Knowing that released individuals will be supervised closely by the MCCJTP case manager, judges have reportedly been active and enthusiastic participants in the diversion program.

More recently, Wicomico's MCCJTP advisory board has focused its attention on prearrest diversion. In 1996 the Wicomico County Detention Center, in collaboration with the county health department, received Edward Byrne Memorial State and Local Law Enforcement Assistance Program funds to establish a mobile crisis unit. With assistance from the GAINS Center, county planners visited mobile crisis programs in Birmingham, Alabama, and Albany, New York. "I came back really enthused," says M. Kirk Daugherty, Chief Deputy in the Wicomico County Sheriff's Office, about his visit to Albany. "It's always nice to hear from a guy who's done a program already. We started our unit in October of 1997 and it's been very beneficial."

Staffed by a deputy sheriff and two case managers (one on call 24 hours a day; one working 2–10 p.m.), Wicomico's mobile crisis unit is always available to help the sheriff's office identify the most appropriate placement for mentally ill individuals. If law enforcement officers responding to an incident involving a mentally ill person determine that criminal charges do not need to be filed, other options (e.g., for shelter or emergency room evaluation) are pursued. The case manager accompanies the mentally ill individual to the agreed-upon destination, thereby relieving law enforcement officers of time-consuming interactions with the health and mental health systems and ensuring that the mentally ill individual has a mental health advocate at his or her side.

Commenting on the kinds of situations that prompt calls to the mobile crisis unit, Daugherty says, "Down here, citizens call the police for everything—marriage counseling—the whole gamut. In situations involving the mentally ill, there may not be a crime, but an emergency petition [to the court to send someone to a State mental health facility] probably won't work either. For instance, one time we had a guy who wasn't taking his meds and was very depressed, but there was nothing we could do. The hospital wouldn't take him. So we called mobile crisis and they relieved our people and surely made the family feel a whole lot better. I like it [mobile crisis] as a safety net. It gives our people more confidence that the [mentally ill] person won't do anything crazy when we're gone. It's a very valuable tool."

Training

Providing training for both criminal justice and mental health professionals is a key objective of most local advisory boards and MHA. With assistance from the GAINS Center and the Virginia Addictions Technology Transfer Center, MHA offers regional cross-trainings for professionals involved in the criminal justice, mental health, and substance abuse treatment systems. The aim of these trainings is to have professionals from the three disciplines learn each other's terminology and understand each other's job duties, roles, and responsibilities. Individual counties have also participated in training and technical assistance offered by the GAINS Center and the

National Institute of Corrections Jails Division. In addition, some counties have developed their own training modules.

Program evaluation

During the past 4 years, State and local planners have concentrated on program development; with funding from two Federal grants, they are now able to focus attention on evaluating service delivery and client outcomes.

Creating a client tracking system and research database. Eight pilot jurisdictions are working with MHA staff and researchers at the University of Maryland at Baltimore to develop a client-tracking system that will assess service provision and individual client outcomes.[22] After helping to create a uniform data-collection instrument, MCCJTP case managers at each pilot site began entering data in April 1998. The database will include intake, aftercare planning, and community follow-up information on each MCCJTP client.[23] It will provide data on the characteristics of clients who receive MCCJTP services; the types and amounts of services MCCJTP clients actually use, both in jail and in the community; the costs of services; and changes in client circumstances within the jail and in the community (e.g., regarding housing, employment, psychiatric hospitalization, arrest, or substance abuse treatment).

Studying the prebooking diversion of mentally ill women offenders. In July 1998 Wicomico County launched an experimental prearrest diversion program for women with co-occurring severe mental illness and substance use disorders who face arrest for a misdemeanor or nonviolent programs funded nationally by SAMHSA's Center for Substance Abuse Treatment and Center for Mental Health Services. Called the Phoenix Project, Wicomico County's program builds on MCCJTP networks to offer 24-hour mobile crisis services, secure crisis housing for women and their children, an integrated outpatient treatment program, case management services with client-to-staff ratios of 20 to 1, and transitional housing for women and their children.

Participants in the study are being assigned randomly to the prebooking intervention or to the standard MCCJTP (postbooking) services available through the Wicomico County Detention Center. Women in the intervention group are being recruited into the program prior to arrest but after determination by law enforcement officers that a complaint is chargeable as a misdemeanor or nonviolent felony. Interview data on women in the intervention group will be compared with similar data collected from women involved in the county's postbooking MCCJTP program. Both process and outcome data will be analyzed to evaluate service provision and client-level outcomes (i.e., recidivism, use of treatment and support services, residential stability, time spent with children, psychiatric symptomology, and level of substance use). Additional analyses involving the pre- and postbooking samples will focus on individual recovery processes, costs, and child outcomes (i.e., social and behavioral functioning and self-concept).

Sustaining Funding: An Ongoing Challenge
With its substantial base of State and Federal funding and with matching funds and in-kind services from many local providers, MCCJTP has been able to serve a large number of mentally ill offenders in jail and in the community. But sustaining financial support is an ever-present challenge.

A key concern is whether local governments will, in the future, assume responsibility for funding services that are now provided with Federal grant monies. In this regard, some MCCJTP advisory board members believe that program evaluation will be essential in persuading local legislators to make a financial commitment to MCCJTP.

A second concern is that MCCJTP funds from MHA have remained capped at $50,000 per site since the Jail Mental Health Program pilots were launched in 1993. Yet with increased costs due to inflation, and with improved identification of mentally ill offenders, those funds cover less of the actual program expenses each year, resulting in increased administrative burdens for participating agencies. Thus far, those agencies have determined that the increases in efficiency and the improved care provided by MCCJTP offset any additional operating expenses it creates.

Finally, like many other States, Maryland has adopted a managed public mental health care system. Prior to its implementation in July 1997, some State and local MCCJTP participants expressed concern that indigent clients might be "lost" in the new fee-for-service system and that compensation might not be adequate to allow providers to respond to the diverse—and often extreme—needs of mentally ill offenders. Some feared that if services were substantially reduced, mentally ill offenders would be sent back into local detention centers and mental institutions.

So far, there is reason for optimism. Because MHA has continued to provide grant funds for MCCJTP, which offers support services that are not covered under managed care (i.e., screening and case management services for jailed mentally ill inmates and community followup for released offenders), mentally ill offenders do not experience interruptions in treatment. When mentally ill offenders are released from jail, they are linked immediately with community-based mental health care providers, ensuring a smooth transition to the managed care system. MCCJTP case managers and other providers involved in the program then continue to work together to provide mentally ill offenders with the full complement of community-based services they require.

Tallying the Accomplishments

Ray Carver smiles as he prepares a pot of spaghetti in his apartment. He is proud that he has food in his refrigerator and a safe place to live. Out of jail for 6 months, Ray now works in the kitchen at Go-Getters and participates in life- and social-skills classes there. He is also preparing for his general equivalency diploma. He attends Alcoholics Anonymous meetings nightly and has regular appointments with a psychiatrist at the county health center. He reports monthly to his probation officer. Ray appreciates the support that he has received from his MCCJTP case manager and other program participants, saying, "In 45 years, this is the only time that people have really cared—have helped me, believed in me, and really supported me. I was tired of the life I was living, but before this, I had no one to turn to for real help."

When the MCCJTP pilot programs were launched in 1993, program planners had several goals. By improving the treatment of mentally ill offenders in jails and in the community, they hoped to improve the quality of care those offenders received, decrease the disruption mentally ill offenders created in correctional and community settings, reduce "system cycling" by coordinating services, and help mentally ill offenders live productively in the community. Five years later, through the dedication of local advisory boards, the commitment of case managers and community-based service providers, and the support of MHA, jurisdictions throughout Maryland have constructed a framework for achieving these goals. The result, as summarized by Charlie Messmer, a substance abuse counselor in Washington County, is that "treatment of mentally ill offenders has become an 'our' problem rather than 'mine' or 'yours.'"

Perhaps the most dramatic changes have occurred in detention centers around the State. Local corrections professionals report that early identification and treatment have reduced inmates' disruptive behavior, training has improved the ability of correctional officers to identify and refer mentally ill inmates for screening, and correctional officers now feel supported by treatment professionals in the jail. According to Barry Stanton, Warden of the Frederick County Detention Center, "These changes have made me feel a whole lot more relaxed. Mentally ill offenders are no longer the primary issue on my desk."

Other criminal justice professionals have also benefited from MCCJTP. Judges and assistant State's attorneys have the assurance that treatment plans will be closely monitored in the community and can rely on case managers for careful assessments of community placements and individual performance. Defense counsels are reassured that clients who are confined in local detention centers receive better care and treatment than in the past and that MCCJTP case managers are able to provide information helpful to making decisions regarding diversion, pretrial release, and case disposition. Probation and parole officers receive support from MCCJTP case managers, who monitor and report on the progress of mentally ill clients in fulfilling their aftercare and treatment plans.

MCCJTP appears also to have dramatically changed the lives of individual clients. Although only careful evaluation of service delivery and case outcomes will demonstrate whether MCCJTP services significantly reduce recidivism, case managers around the State report that some MCCJTP clients have made substantial progress in improving the quality of their lives and contributing to the communities in which they live. As Maureen Plunkert, a case manager in Wicomico County, remarked, "Amazing personalities are revealed as these men and women start getting well."

Sources for More Information

The Maryland Department of Health and Mental Hygiene's Division of Specific Populations fosters the development of innovative programs for recipients of mental health services with special needs, such as individuals with psychiatric disabilities who are homeless, are in jail but could be appropriately served in the community, have co-occurring substance abuse disorders, and/or are deaf. The Division of Specific Populations sponsors MCCJTP. For more information, contact:

Joan Gillece Assistant Director
Division of Specific Populations, Mental Hygiene Administration
201 West Preston Street Baltimore, MD 21201
Telephone: 410–767–6603
TTY: 410–767–6539
Fax: 410–333–5402

The National Institute of Justice (NIJ) is the principal research, evaluation, and development agency of the U.S. Department of Justice (DOJ). For information about NIJ's efforts in corrections and program development, contact:

Marilyn C. Moses Program Analyst
National Institute of Justice
810 Seventh Street N.W., 7th Floor
Washington, DC 20531
Telephone: 202–514–6205
Fax: 202–307–6256

E-mail: moses@ojp.usdoj.gov

The National Criminal Justice Reference Service (NCJRS) was established by NIJ in 1972. It serves as the national and international clearinghouse for the exchange of criminal justice information. For more information about topical searches, bibliographies, custom searches, and other available services, contact:

NCJRS
P.O. Box 6000
Rockville, MD 20849–6000
Telephone: 800–851–3420 (8:30 a.m. to 7 **p.m. Eastern time, Monday through Friday) E-mail: askncjrs@ncjrs.org**

The Bureau of Justice Assistance (BJA), a component of DOJ's Office of Justice Programs, supports innovative programs that strengthen the Nation's criminal justice system by assisting State and local governments in combating violent crime and drug abuse.

BJA primarily makes funding available through the Edward Byrne Memorial State and Local Law Enforcement Assistance Program. Under this program, BJA is authorized to make formula grants to States and territories, which award subgrants to local units of government. States are required to contribute a 25-percent cash match toward overall funding. For more information, contact:

Mary Santonastasso
Director, State and Local Assistance Division Bureau of Justice Assistance
810 Seventh Street N.W., 4th Floor Washington, DC 20531
Telephone: 202–305–2088
Fax: 202–514–5956

E-mail: santonas@ojp.usdoj.gov

The American Jail Association (AJA) provides regional training seminars, onsite technical assistance, and training materials related to inmate programming, direct supervision, and other corrections topics for a modest fee. The Association also sponsors an Annual Training Conference & Jail Expo. Contact:

Stephen J. Ingley Executive Director American Jail Association 2053 Day Road, Suite 100
Hagerstown, MD 21740–9795
Telephone: 301–790–3930
Fax: 301–790–2941
E-mail: aja@corrections.com World Wide Web site: http:// www.corrections.com/aja

The National Institute of Corrections (NIC) Jails Division coordinates services to improve the management and operation of jail systems throughout the United States and its commonwealths and territories. Technical assistance, training, and information are pro- vided in many areas, including medical and mental health services and suicide prevention. For more information on technical assistance and training activities, contact:

NIC Jails Division
1960 Industrial Circle, Suite A Longmont, CO 80501
Telephone: 800–995–6429
Fax: 303–682–0469

HUD's Shelter Plus Care program provides rental assistance in connection with support services from other providers to homeless people with disabilities. The program allows for a variety of housing choices, such as group homes or individual units, coupled with a range of supportive services funded by other sources. Grantees must match the rental assistance with supportive services that are at least equal in value to the amount of HUD's rental assistance. States, local governments, and public housing agencies may apply. HUD awards Shelter Plus Care funds as annual competitive grants. For more information, contact:

Allison Manning
U.S. Department of Housing and Urban Development
Office of Community Planning and Development
Office of Special Needs Assistance Programs 451 Seventh Street S.W.
Washington, DC 20410
Telephone: 202–708–0614, ext. 4497

The Substance Abuse and Mental Health Services Administration (SAMHSA) is part of the U.S. Department of Health and Human Services. Its mission is to improve the quality and availability of prevention, treatment, and rehabilitation services to reduce the illness, death, disability, and cost to society that result from substance abuse and mental illness. SAMHSA comprises the Center for Mental Health Services (CMHS), the Center for Substance Abuse Prevention (CSAP), and the Center for Substance Abuse Treatment (CSAT). The **Phoenix Project,** which involves the pre-arrest diversion of mentally ill women offenders in Wicomico County, MD, is funded jointly by CMHS and CSAT under the Federal **Knowledge Development and Application Program.** For more information on that program, contact:

Susan Salasin
Director of Mental Health and Criminal Justice Programs
Center for Mental Health Services 5600 Fishers Lane, Room 11C–26
Rockville, MD 20857
Telephone: 301–443–6127
Fax: 301–443–0541

E-mail: ssalasin@samhsa.gov

CSAT Office of Communications and External Liaison
5600 Fishers Lane, 6th Floor
Rockville, MD 20857
Telephone: 301–443–5052
Fax: 301–443–7801

Established in 1995, the **National GAINS Center for People With Co-Occurring Disorders in the Justice System** serves as a national locus for the collection and dissemination of information about effective mental health and substance abuse services for people with co-occurring disorders who come in contact with the justice system. The GAINS Center is a Federal partnership between NIC and the Office of Justice Programs within the U.S. Department of Justice and CSAT and CMHS within the U.S. Department of Health and Human Services. The GAINS Center is operated by Policy Research, Inc., through a cooperative agreement with the Federal partners that is administered by NIC. For more information, contact:

The GAINS Center Policy Research, Inc. 262 Delaware Avenue
Delmar, NY 12054 Telephone: 800–311–GAIN
Fax: 518–439–7612

Projects for Assistance in Transition from Homelessness (PATH) is part of the Mental Health Services Block Grant to the States that is overseen by SAMHSA's CMHS. PATH provides a variety of treatment formula grant awards to States for homeless people with mental illnesses and co-occurring substance use problems. Services covered include treatment, support services in residential settings, and coordination of services and housing. For more information, contact:

Center for Mental Health Services Homeless Programs Branch
5600 Fishers Lane, Room 11C–05 Rockville, MD 20857
Telephone: 301–443–3706
Fax: 301–443–0256

Funded by SAMHSA, the **Virginia Addiction Technology Transfer Center** has developed a 1-week cross-training curriculum on offenders with co-occurring disorders. Offered to corrections officers, substance abuse counselors, and mental health treatment counselors, the training consists of 15 modules that may be used separately or in conjunction with each other as needed. For more information, contact:

Scott Reiner
Criminal Justice Coordinator
Virginia Addiction Technology Transfer Center
Division of Substance Abuse Medicine Medical College of Virginia
1112 East Clay Street
Box 980205
Richmond, VA 23298–0205
Telephone: 800–828–8323
Fax: 804–828–9906

NIJ Publications on Offender Health Care and Transitional Services

The National Institute of Justice has sponsored a number of publications related to the issue of offender health care and transitional services. To get a free copy of these publications, write the National Criminal Justice Reference Service, P.O. Box 6000, Rockville, MD 20849–6000; call them at 800–851–3420; or send e-mail to *askncjrs@ncjrs.org*.

Case Management in the Criminal Justice System, Research in Action, 1999 (NCJ 173409).

The Women's Prison Association: Supporting Women Offenders and Their Families, Program Focus, 1998 (NCJ 172858).

The Delaware Department of Correction Life Skills Program. Program Focus, 1998 (NCJ 169589).

Chicago's Safer Foundation: A Road Back for Ex-Offenders, Program Focus, 1998 (NCJ 167575).

Texas' Project RIO (Re-Integration of Offenders), Program Focus, 1998 (NCJ 168637).

Successful Job Placement for Ex-Offenders: The Center for Employment Opportunities, Program Focus, 1998 (NCJ 168102).

Providing Services for Jail Inmates With Mental Disorders, Research in Brief, 1997 (NCJ 162207).

The Orange County, Florida, Jail Educational and Vocational Programs, Program Focus, 1997 (NCJ 166820)

The Effectiveness of Treatment for Drug Abusers Under Criminal Justice Supervision, Research Report, 1995 (NCJ 157642).

Evaluation of Drug Treatment in Local Corrections, Research Report, 1997 (NCJ 159313).

The Americans With Disabilities Act and Criminal Justice: Mental Disabilities and Corrections, Research in Action, 1995 (NCJ 155061).

Managing Mentally Ill Offenders in the Community: Milwaukee's Community Support Program, Program Focus, 1994 (NCJ 145330).

Notes

1. Ray Carver's history is a composite of those reported to the author in interviews with 14 Maryland Community Criminal Justice Treatment Program participants.

2. Harlow, C.W., *Profile of Jail Inmates 1996,* Bureau of Justice Statistics Special Report, Washington, DC: U.S. Department of Justice, Bureau of Justice Statistics, April 1998, NCJ 164620. In 1996, there were 507,026 jail inmates. Men were less likely than women to have ever been treated for a mental or emotional problem. The author notes that 24 percent of male inmates and 36 percent of female inmates reported having received mental health services.

3. Ibid., 12.

4. Palermo, G.B., M.B. Smith, F.J. Liska, "Jails Versus Mental Hospitals: A Social Dilemma," *International Journal of Offender Therapy and Comparative Criminology* 35 (2) (Summer 1991): 97–106; Judiscak, Daniel L., "Why Are the Mentally Ill in Jail?" *American Jails* (November–December 1995): 11–15.

5. National Coalition for Jail Reform, *Removing the Chronically Mentally Ill From Jail: Case Studies of Collaboration Between Local Criminal Justice and Mental Health Systems,* Rockville, MD: U.S. Department of Health and Human Services, National Institute of Mental Health, 1984; Janik, J., "Dealing With Mentally Ill Offenders," *Law Enforcement Bulletin* 61 (7) (July 1992): 22–26.

6. Haddad, J., "Managing the Special Needs of Mentally Ill Inmates," *American Jails* 7 (1) (March-April 1993): 62–65; National Coalition for Jail Reform, *Removing the Chronically Mentally Ill From Jail: Case Studies of Collaboration Between Local Criminal Justice and Mental*

Health Systems; The Center on Crime, Communities and Culture, *Mental Illness in U.S. Jails: Diverting the Nonviolent, Low-Level Offender,* Research Brief, Occasional Paper Series, No.1, New York: The Center on Crime, Communities and Culture, November 1996.

7. Wilberg, J.K., K. Matyniak, and A. Cohen, "Milwaukee County Task Force on the Incarceration of Mentally Ill Persons," *American Jails* (Summer 1989): 20–26; Snow, W.H., and K.H. Briar, "The Convergence of the Mentally Disordered and the Jail Population," in *The Clinical Treatment of the Criminal Offender in Outpatient Mental Health Settings,* ed. N.J. Palone and S. Chaneles, New York: The Haworth Press, 1990: 147–162; Torrey, E.F., J. Stieber, J. Ezekiel, S.M. Wolfe, J. Sharfstein, J.H. Noble, and L.M. Flynn, *Criminalizing the Seriously Mentally Ill: The Abuse of Jails as Mental Hospitals,* Washington, DC: Public Citizen's Health Research Group, 1992; Landsberg, G. "Developing Comprehensive Mental Health Services in Local Jails and Police Lockups," in *Innovations in Community Mental Health,* ed. S. Cooper and T.H. Lentner, Sarasota, FL: Professional Resource Press, 1992: 97–123.

8. See for example, *Estelle* v. *Gamble,* 429 U.S. 97 (1976); *Bell* v. *Wolfish,* 441 U.S. 535, n.16, 545 (1979); *Bowring* v. *Godwin,* 551 F.2d 44 (4th Cir 1977).

9. Snow, W.H., and K.H. Briar, "The Convergence of the Mentally Disordered and the Jail Population"; Steadman, H.J., S.M. Morris, D.L. Dennis, "The Diversion of Mentally Ill Persons From Jails to Community-Based Services: A Profile of Programs," *American Journal of Public Health* 85 (12) (December 1995): 1630–1635. For more information on existing models for screening and linking mentally ill jail detainees with community-based services, see Veysey, B.M., H.J. Steadman, J.P. Morrissey, and M. Johnson, "In Search of the Missing Linkages: Continuity of Care in U.S. Jails," *Behavioral Sciences and the Law* 15 (1997): 383–397, in which the authors discuss program strategies in seven city and county jails.

10. Steadman, H., and B. Veysey, *Providing Services for Jail Inmates With Mental Disorders,* Research in Brief, Washington, DC: U.S. Department of Justice, National Institute of Justice, April 1997, NCJ 162207; Muzekari, L.H., E.E. Morissey, and A. Young, "Community Mental Health Centers and County Jails: Divergent Perspectives?" *American Jails* XI (1) (March–April 1997): 50–52.

11. Teplin, L.A., K.M. Abram, and G.M. McClelland, "Mentally Disordered Women in Jail: Who Receives Services?" *American Journal of Public Health* 87 (4) (1997): 604–609.

12. Steadman and Vesey, *Providing Services for Jail Inmates With Mental Disorders,* 5.

13. Correctional Association of New York, *Insane and in Jail: The Need for Treatment Options for the Mentally Ill in New York's County Jails,* New York: Correctional Association of New York, October, 1989; Abram, K., and L. Teplin, "Co-Occurring Disorders Among Mentally Ill Jail Detainees," *American Psychologist* 46 (10) (October 1991): 1036–1045; Peters, R.H., W.D. Kearns, M.R. Murrin, and A.S. Donente, "Psychopathology and Mental Health Needs Among Drug- Involved Inmates," *Journal of Prison and Jail Health* 11 (1) (Summer 1992): 3–25; Martell, D.A., R. Rosner, and R.B.I. Harmon, "Base-Rate Estimates of Criminal Behavior by Homeless Mentally Ill Persons in New York City," *Psychiatric Services* 46 (6) (June 1995): 596–601; Gillece, J., "An Analysis of Health, Criminal Justice, and Social Service Utilization by Individuals Hospitalized, Incarcerated, or Homeless," unpublished doctoral dissertation, College Park: University of Maryland, 1996: 2–42.

14. Gillece, J., "An Analysis of Health, Criminal Justice, and Social Service Utilization by Individuals Hospitalized, Incarcerated, or Homeless," 4.

15. The following counties participate in MCCJTP: Allegany, Anne Arundel, Baltimore, Calvert, Caroline, Carroll, Cecil, Charles, Dorchester, Frederick, Harford, Kent,

Prince Georges, Queen Annes, St. Marys, Washington, Wicomico, and Worcester. Several of these commenced program planning in February 1997.

16. Precise administrative cost figures are not available. In each jurisdiction, a portion of supervisory, fiscal, and secretarial staff hours are contributed to support MCCJTP staff. These costs are thought to vary considerably across jurisdictions because of variation in pay scales and in the complexity of MCCJTP programs.

17. Governor's Office of Justice Administration, *Report of the State/Local Criminal Justice/ Mental Health Task Force*, Baltimore, MD: Governor's Office of Justice Administration, January 1995: 12.

18. The GAINS Center is run by Policy Research, Inc., a not-for-profit branch of Policy Research Associates in Delmar, NY, a research firm studying issues in mental health, substance abuse, criminal justice, and homelessness.

19. As might be expected, not all mentally ill individuals who are counseled in detention centers agree to take part in community- based followup. Case managers report that some individuals participate only after they fail repeatedly to make it on their own.

20. To ensure sufficient numbers of participants, the target population was subsequently expanded to include parolees and probationers on intensive supervision caseloads and participants in PATH, a Federal formula grant program that funds outreach, case management, mental health, and substance abuse services for homeless individuals with serious mental illness and/or co-occurring substance use disorders.

21. These include Baltimore, Calvert, Caroline, Dorchester, Frederick, Kent, and Queen Annes counties. The counties provide a 25-percent cash match.

22. Seven of the counties—Baltimore, Calvert, Caroline, Kent, Queen Annes, Dorchester, and Frederick—receive Edward Byrne Memorial State and Local Law

Enforcement Assistance Program funds to aid dually diagnosed offenders. That funding also supports the 3-year database development and research effort. In addition, Wicomico County has been included among the pilot sites. Data collection in that county will aid in the evaluation of the Phoenix Project.

23. The tracking database has three modules. The Intake Module includes information on each client's demographic characteristics, current living situation, family history, employment and finances, prior alcohol and drug use, alcohol and drug treatment history, prior psychiatric treatment, medical treatment, and legal circumstances. Two standardized instruments—the Multnomah County Community Abilities Scale, which assesses a client's level of social functioning across multiple life domains and the Lehman Quality of Life Interview (TL–30S), which includes objective and subjective measures of quality of life across eight life domains—are also included in the intake data module. The Service Encounter Module includes information on the type, amount, and duration of services provided to jail-based clients. This module will support analysis of level of services and service costs. The Aftercare Module includes data on the aftercare service plan, client contacts with referral agencies, and self-reported changes in client circumstances (e.g., in residence, employment, psychiatric hospitalization, arrests, and substance abuse treatment). This Program Focus was written by Catherine Conly, Associate at Abt Associates Inc. In preparing the report, Ms. Conly met at length with Joan Gillece and other staff of Maryland's Mental Hygiene Administration. She also interviewed officials who participate in the MCCJTP programs in Allegany, Charles, Frederick, Washington, and Wicomico counties; observed local advisory board meetings; and interviewed MCCJTP clients both in jails and in the community. In addition, Ms. Conly participated in a 3-day, multisite cross-training for mental health, substance abuse, and corrections professionals involved in the MCCJTP.

Findings and conclusions of the research reported here are those of the author and do not necessarily reflect the official position or policies of the U.S. Department of Justice.

Discussion Question

Do you believe criminal justice practitioners should be involved in projects such as this? Why or why not?

Critical Thinking Exercise

The critical thinking exercise for this chapter is to actually write up a critical thinking exercise that demonstrates your knowledge of the materials in this reading as well as more comprehensively for the course.

THE DREAM OF A RIDICULOUS MAN

By

Fyodor Dostoyevsky

I am a ridiculous person. Now they call me a madman. That would be a promotion if it were not that I remain as ridiculous in their eyes as before. But now I do not resent it, they are all dear to me now, even when they laugh at me—and, indeed, it is just then that they are particularly dear to me. I could join in their laughter—not exactly at myself, but through affection for them, if I did not feel so sad as I look at them. Sad because they do not know the truth and I do know it. Oh, how hard it is to be the only one who knows the truth! But they won't understand that. No, they won't understand it.

In old days I used to be miserable at seeming ridiculous. Not seeming, but being. I have always been ridiculous, and I have known it, perhaps, from the hour I was born. Perhaps from the time I was seven years old I knew I was ridiculous. Afterwards I went to school, studied at the university, and, do you know, the more I learned, the more thoroughly I understood that I was ridiculous. So that it seemed in the end as though all the sciences I studied at the university existed only to prove and make evident to me as I went more deeply into them that I was ridiculous. It was the same with life as it was with science. With every year the same consciousness of the ridiculous figure I cut in every relation grew and strengthened. Everyone always laughed at me. But not one of them knew or guessed that if there were one man on earth who knew better than anybody else that I was absurd, it was myself, and what I resented most of all was that they did not know that.

But that was my own fault; I was so proud that nothing would have ever induced me to tell it to anyone. This pride grew in me with the years; and if it had happened that I allowed myself to confess to any one that I was ridiculous, I believe that I should have blown out my brains the same evening. Oh, how I suffered in my early youth from the fear that I might give way and confess it to my schoolfellows.

But since I grew to manhood, I have for some unknown reason become calmer, though I realised my awful characteristic more fully every year. I say "unknown," for to this day I cannot tell why it was. Perhaps it was owing to the terrible misery that was growing in my soul through something which was of more consequence than anything else about me: that something was the conviction that had come upon me that *nothing in the world mattered*. I had long had an inkling of it, but the full realisation came last year almost suddenly. I suddenly felt that it was all the same to me whether the world existed or whether there had never been anything at all: I began to feel with all my being that there was *nothing existing*.

At first I fancied that many things had existed in the past, but afterwards I guessed that there never had been anything in the past either, but that it had only seemed so for some reason. Little by little I guessed that there would be nothing in the future either. Then I left off being angry with people and almost ceased to notice them. Indeed this showed itself even in the pettiest trifles: I used, for instance, to knock against people in the street. And not so much from being lost in thought: what had I to think about? I had almost given up thinking by that time; nothing mattered to me. If at least I had solved my problems! Oh, I had not settled one of them, and how many they were! But I gave up caring about anything, and all the problems disappeared.

And it was after that that I found out the truth. I learnt the truth last November—on the third of November, to be precise—and I remember every instant since. It was a gloomy evening, one of the gloomiest possible evenings. I was going home at about eleven o'clock, and I remember that I thought that the evening could not be gloomier. Even physically. Rain had been falling all day, and it had been a cold, gloomy, almost menacing rain, with, I remember, an unmistakable spite against mankind. Suddenly between ten and eleven it had stopped, and was followed by a horrible dampness, colder and damper than the rain, and a sort of steam was rising from everything, from every stone in the street, and from every by-lane if one looked down it as far as one could.

A thought suddenly occurred to me, that if all the street lamps had been put out it would have been less cheerless, that the gas made one's heart sadder because it lighted it all up. I had had scarcely any dinner that day, and had been spending the evening with an engineer, and two other friends had been there also. I sat silent—I fancy I bored them. They talked of something rousing and suddenly they got excited over it. But they did not really care, I could see that, and only made a show of being excited. I suddenly said as much to them. "My friends," I said, "you really do not care one way or the other." They were not offended, but they all laughed at me. That was because I spoke without any note of reproach, simply because it did not matter to me. They saw it did not, and it amused them.

As I was thinking about the gas lamps in the street I looked up at the sky. The sky was horribly dark, but one could distinctly see tattered clouds, and between them fathomless black patches. Suddenly I noticed in one of these patches a star, and began watching it intently. That was because that star gave me an idea: I decided to kill myself that night. I had firmly determined to do so two months before, and poor as I was, I bought a splendid revolver that very day, and loaded it. But two months had passed and it was still lying in my drawer; I was so utterly indifferent that I wanted to seize a moment when I would not be so indifferent—why, I don't know. And so for two months every night that I came home I thought I would shoot myself. I kept waiting for the right moment. And so now this star gave me a thought. I made up my mind that it should certainly be that night. And why the star gave me the thought I don't know.

And just as I was looking at the sky, this little girl took me by the elbow. The street was empty, and there was scarcely any one to be seen. A cabman was sleeping in the distance in his cab. It was a child of eight with a kerchief on her head, wearing nothing but a wretched little dress all soaked with rain, but I noticed particularly her wet broken shoes and I recall them now. They caught my eye particularly. She suddenly pulled me by the elbow and called me. She was not weeping, but was spasmodically crying out some words which she could not utter properly, because she was shivering and shuddering all over.

She was in terror about something, and kept crying, "Mammy, mammy!" I turned facing her, I did not say a word and went on; but she ran, pulling at me, and there was that note in her voice which in frightened children means despair. I know that sound. Though she did not articulate the words, I understood that her mother was dying, or that something of the sort was happening to them, and that she had run out to call someone, to find something to help her mother. I did not go with her; on the contrary, I had an impulse to drive her away. I told her first to go to a policeman. But clasping her hands, she ran beside me sobbing and gasping, and would not leave me. Then I stamped my foot, and shouted at her. She called out "Sir! sir!..." but suddenly abandoned me and rushed headlong across the road. Some other passer-by appeared there, and she evidently flew from me to him.

I mounted up to my fifth storey. I have a room in a flat where there are other lodgers. My room is small and poor, with a garret window in the shape of a semicircle. I have a sofa covered with American leather, a table with books on it, two chairs and a comfortable arm-chair, as old as old can be, but of the good old-fashioned shape. I sat down, lighted the candle, and began thinking. In the room next to mine, through the partition wall, a perfect Bedlam was going on. It had been going on for the last three days.

A retired captain lived there, and he had half a dozen visitors, gentlemen of doubtful reputation, drinking vodka and playing *stoss* with old cards. The night before there had been a fight, and I know that two of them had been for a long time engaged in dragging each other about by the hair. The landlady wanted to complain, but she was in abject terror of the captain. There was only one other lodger in the flat, a thin little regimental lady, on a visit to Petersburg, with three little children who had been taken ill since they came into the lodgings.

Both she and her children were in mortal fear of the captain, and lay trembling and crossing themselves all night, and the youngest child had a sort of fit from fright. That captain, I know for a fact, sometimes stops people in the Nevsky Prospect and begs. They won't take him into the service, but strange to say (that's why I am telling this), all this month that the captain has been here his behaviour has caused me no annoyance. I have, of course, tried to avoid his acquaintance from the very beginning, and he, too, was bored with me from the first; but I never care how much they shout the other side of the partition nor how many of them there are in there: I sit up all night and forget them so completely that I do not even hear them. I stay awake till daybreak, and have been going on like that for the last year.

I sit up all night in my arm-chair at the table, doing nothing. I only read by day. I sit—don't even think; ideas of a sort wander through my mind and I let them come and go as they will. A whole candle is burnt every night. I sat down quietly at the table, took out the revolver and put it down before me. When I had put it down I asked myself, I remember, "Is that so?" and answered with complete conviction, "It is." That is, I shall shoot myself. I knew that I should shoot myself that night for certain, but how much longer I should go on sitting at the table I did not know. And no doubt I should have shot myself if it had not been for that little girl.

II

You see, though nothing mattered to me, I could feel pain, for instance. If anyone had struck me it would have hurt me. It was the same morally: if anything very pathetic happened, I should have felt pity just as I used to do in old days when there were things in life that did matter to me. I had felt pity that evening. I should have certainly helped a child. Why, then, had I not helped the little girl? Because of an idea that occurred to me at the time: when she was calling and pulling at me, a question suddenly arose before me and I could not settle it. The question was an idle one, but I was vexed. I was vexed at the reflection that if I were going to make an end of myself that night, nothing in life ought to have mattered to me.

Why was it that all at once I did not feel that nothing mattered and was sorry for the little girl? I remember that I was very sorry for her, so much so that I felt a strange pang, quite incongruous in my position. Really I do not know better how to convey my fleeting sensation at the moment, but the sensation persisted at home when I was sitting at the table, and I was very much irritated as I had not been for a long time past. One reflection followed another. I saw clearly that so long as I was still a human being and not nothingness, I was alive and so could suffer, be angry and feel shame at my actions. So be it. But if I am going to kill myself, in two hours, say, what is the little girl to me and what have I to do with shame or with anything else in the world? I shall turn into nothing, absolutely nothing.

And can it really be true that the consciousness that I shall *completely* cease to exist immediately and so everything else will cease to exist, does not in the least affect my feeling of pity for the child nor the feeling of shame after a contemptible action? I stamped and shouted at the unhappy child as though to say—not only I feel no pity, but even if I behave inhumanly and contemptibly, I am free to, for in another two hours everything will be extinguished. Do you believe that that was why I shouted that? I am almost convinced of it now. It seemed clear to me that life and the world somehow depended upon me now.

I may almost say that the world now seemed created for me alone: if I shot myself the world would cease to be at least for me. I say nothing of its being likely that nothing will exist for any one when I am gone, and that as soon as my consciousness is extinguished the whole world will vanish too and become void like a phantom, as a mere appurtenance of my consciousness, for possibly all this world and all these people are only me myself. I remember that as I sat and reflected, I turned all these new questions that swarmed one after another quite the other way, and thought of something quite new.

For instance, a strange reflection suddenly occurred to me, that if I had lived before on the moon or on Mars and there had committed the most disgraceful and dishonourable action and had there been put to such shame and ignominy as one can only conceive and realise in dreams, in nightmares, and if, finding myself afterwards on earth, I were able to retain the memory of what I had done on the other planet and at the same time knew that I should never, under any circumstances, return there, then looking from the earth to the moon—*should I care or not?* Should I feel shame for that action or not? These were idle and superfluous questions for the revolver was already lying before me, and I knew in every fibre of my being that it would happen for certain, but they excited me and I raged. I could not die now without having first settled something.

In short, the child had saved me, for I put off my pistol shot for the sake of these questions. Meanwhile the clamour had begun to subside in the captain's room: they had finished their game, were settling down to sleep, and meanwhile were grumbling and languidly winding up their quarrels. At that point I suddenly fell asleep in my chair at the table—a thing which had never happened to me before. I dropped asleep quite unawares.

Dreams, as we all know, are very queer things: some parts are presented with appalling vividness, with details worked up with the elaborate finish of jewellery, while others one gallops through, as it were, without noticing them at all, as, for instance, through space and time. Dreams seem to be spurred on not by reason but by desire, not by the head but by the heart, and yet what complicated tricks my reason has played sometimes in dreams, what utterly incomprehensible things happen to it!

My brother died five years ago, for instance. I sometimes dream of him; he takes part in my affairs, we are very much interested, and yet all through my dream I quite know and remember that my brother is dead and buried. How is it that I am not surprised that, though he is dead, he is here beside me and working with me? Why is it that my reason fully accepts it? But enough.

I will begin about my dream. Yes, I dreamed a dream, my dream of the third of November. They tease me now, telling me it was only a dream. But does it matter whether it was a dream or reality, if the dream made known to me the truth? If once one has recognised the truth and seen it, you know that it is the truth and that there is no other and there cannot be, whether you are asleep or awake. Let it be a dream, so be it, but that real life of which you make so much I had meant to extinguish by suicide, and my dream, my dream—oh, it revealed to me a different life, renewed, grand and full of power!
Listen.

III

I have mentioned that I dropped asleep unawares and even seemed to be still reflecting on the same subjects. I suddenly dreamt that I picked up the revolver and aimed it straight at my heart—my heart, and not my head; and I had determined beforehand to fire at my head, at my right temple. After aiming at my chest I waited a second or two, and suddenly my candle, my table, and the wall in front of me began moving and heaving. I made haste to pull the trigger.

In dreams you sometimes fall from a height, or are stabbed, or beaten, but you never feel pain unless, perhaps, you really bruise yourself against the bedstead, then you feel pain and almost always wake up from it. It was the same in my dream. I did not feel any pain, but it seemed as though with my shot everything within me was shaken and everything was suddenly dimmed, and it grew horribly black around me.

I seemed to be blinded and benumbed, and I was lying on something hard, stretched on my back; I saw nothing, and could not make the slightest movement. People were walking and shouting around me, the captain bawled, the landlady shrieked—and suddenly another break and I was being carried in a closed coffin. And I felt how the coffin was shaking and reflected upon it, and for the first time the idea struck me that I was dead, utterly dead, I knew it and had no doubt of it, I could neither see nor move and yet I was feeling and reflecting. But I was soon reconciled to the position, and as one usually does in a dream, accepted the facts without disputing them.

And now I was buried in the earth. They all went away, I was left alone, utterly alone. I did not move. Whenever before I had imagined being buried the one sensation I associated with the grave was that of damp and cold. So now I felt that I was very cold, especially the tips of my toes, but I felt nothing else.

I lay still, strange to say I expected nothing, accepting without dispute that a dead man had nothing to expect. But it was damp. I don't know how long a time passed—whether an hour, or several days, or many days. But all at once a drop of water fell on my closed left eye, making its way through a coffin lid; it was followed a minute later by a second, then a minute later by a third—and so on, regularly every minute. There was a sudden glow of profound indignation in my heart, and I suddenly felt in it a pang of physical pain. "That's my wound," I thought; "that's the bullet...." And drop after drop every minute kept falling on my closed eyelid. And all at once, not with my voice, but with my whole being, I called upon the power that was responsible for all that was happening to me:

"Whoever you may be, if you exist, and if anything more rational than what is happening here is possible, suffer it to be here now. But if you are revenging yourself upon me for my senseless suicide by the hideousness and absurdity of this subsequent existence, then let me tell you that no torture could ever equal the contempt which I shall go on dumbly feeling, though my martyrdom may last a million years!"

I made this appeal and held my peace. There was a full minute of unbroken silence and again another drop fell, but I knew with infinite unshakable certainty that everything would change immediately. And behold my grave suddenly was rent asunder, that is, I don't know whether it was opened or dug up, but I was caught up by some dark and unknown being and we found ourselves in space. I suddenly regained my sight. It was the dead of night, and never, never had there been such darkness.

We were flying through space far away from the earth. I did not question the being who was taking me; I was proud and waited. I assured myself that I was not afraid, and was thrilled with ecstasy at the thought that I was not afraid. I do not know how long we were flying, I cannot imagine; it happened as it always does in dreams when you skip over space and time, and the laws of thought and existence, and only pause upon the points for which the heart yearns. I remember that I suddenly saw in the darkness a star. "Is that Sirius?" I asked impulsively, though I had not meant to ask any questions.

"No, that is the star you saw between the clouds when you were coming home," the being who was carrying me replied.

I knew that it had something like a human face. Strange to say, I did not like that being, in fact I felt an intense aversion for it. I had expected complete non-existence, and that was why I had put a bullet through my heart. And here I was in the hands of a creature not human, of course, but yet living, existing. "And so there is life beyond the grave," I thought with the strange frivolity one has in dreams. But in its inmost depth my heart remained unchanged. "And if I have got to exist again," I thought, "and live once more under the control of some irresistible power, I won't be vanquished and humiliated."

"You know that I am afraid of you and despise me for that," I said suddenly to my companion, unable to refrain from the humiliating question which implied a confession, and feeling my humiliation stab my heart as with a pin. He did not answer my question, but all at once I felt that he was not even despising me, but was laughing at me and had no compassion for me, and that our journey had an unknown and mysterious object that concerned me only.

Fear was growing in my heart. Something was mutely and painfully communicated to me from my silent companion, and permeated my whole being. We were flying through dark, unknown space. I had for some time lost sight of the constellations familiar to my eyes. I knew that there were stars in the heavenly spaces the light of which took thousands or millions of years to reach the earth. Perhaps we were already flying through those spaces. I expected something with a terrible anguish that tortured my heart.

And suddenly I was thrilled by a familiar feeling that stirred me to the depths: I suddenly caught sight of our sun! I knew that it could not be *our* sun, that gave life to *our* earth, and that we were an infinite distance from our sun, but for some reason I knew in my whole being that it was a sun exactly like ours, a duplicate of it. A sweet, thrilling feeling resounded with ecstasy in my heart: the kindred power of the same light which had given me light stirred an echo in my heart and awakened it, and I had a sensation of life, the old life of the past for the first time since I had been in the grave.

"But if that is the sun, if that is exactly the same as our sun," I cried, "where is the earth?"

And my companion pointed to a star twinkling in the distance with an emerald light. We were flying straight towards it.

"And are such repetitions possible in the universe? Can that be the law of Nature?... And if that is an earth there, can it be just the same earth as ours ... just the same, as poor, as unhappy, but precious and beloved forever, arousing in the most ungrateful of her children the same poignant love for her that we feel for our earth?" I cried out, shaken by irresistible, ecstatic love for the old familiar earth which I had left. The image of the poor child whom I had repulsed flashed through my mind.

"You shall see it all," answered my companion, and there was a note of sorrow in his voice.

But we were rapidly approaching the planet. It was growing before my eyes; I could already distinguish the ocean, the outline of Europe; and suddenly a feeling of a great and holy jealousy glowed in my heart.

"How can it be repeated and what for? I love and can love only that earth which I have left, stained with my blood, when, in my ingratitude, I quenched my life with a bullet in my heart. But I have never, never ceased to love that earth, and perhaps on the very night I parted from it I loved it more than ever. Is there suffering upon this new earth? On our earth we can only love with suffering and through suffering. We cannot love otherwise, and we know of no other sort of love. I want suffering in order to love. I long, I thirst, this very instant, to kiss with tears the earth that I have left, and I don't want, I won't accept life on any other!"

But my companion had already left me. I suddenly, quite without noticing how, found myself on this other earth, in the bright light of a sunny day, fair as paradise. I believe I was standing on one of the islands that make up on our globe the Greek archipelago, or on the coast of the mainland facing that archipelago. Oh, everything was exactly as it is with us, only everything seemed to have a festive radiance, the splendour of some great, holy triumph attained at last. The caressing sea, green as emerald, splashed softly upon the shore and kissed it with manifest, almost conscious love. The tall, lovely trees stood in all the glory of their blossom, and their innumerable leaves greeted me, I am certain, with their soft, caressing rustle and seemed to articulate words of love. The grass glowed with bright and fragrant flowers. Birds were flying in flocks in the air, and perched fearlessly on my shoulders and arms and joyfully struck me with their darling, fluttering wings.

And at last I saw and knew the people of this happy land. They came to me of themselves, they surrounded me, kissed me. The children of the sun, the children of their sun—oh, how beautiful they were! Never had I seen on our own earth such beauty in mankind. Only perhaps in our children, in their earliest years, one might find some remote, faint reflection of this beauty. The eyes of these happy people shone with a clear brightness. Their faces were radiant with the light of reason and fullness of a serenity that comes of perfect understanding, but those faces were gay; in their words and voices there was a note of childlike joy.

Oh, from the first moment, from the first glance at them, I understood it all! It was the earth untarnished by the Fall; on it lived people who had not sinned. They lived just in such a paradise as that in which, according to all the legends of mankind, our first parents lived before they sinned; the only difference was that all this earth was the same paradise. These people, laughing joyfully, thronged round me and caressed me; they took me home with them, and each of them tried to reassure me. Oh, they asked me no questions, but they seemed, I fancied, to know everything without asking, and they wanted to make haste and smoothe away the signs of suffering from my face.

IV

And do you know what? Well, granted that it was only a dream, yet the sensation of the love of those innocent and beautiful people has remained with me forever, and I feel as though their love is still flowing out to me from over there. I have seen them myself, have known them and been convinced; I loved them, I suffered for them afterwards. Oh, I understood at once even at the time that in many things I could not understand them at all; as an up-to-date Russian progressive and contemptible Petersburger, it struck me as inexplicable that, knowing so much, they had, for instance, no science like ours. But I soon realised that their knowledge was gained and fostered by intuitions different from those of us on earth, and that their aspirations, too, were quite different.

They desired nothing and were at peace; they did not aspire to knowledge of life as we aspire to understand it, because their lives were full. But their knowledge was higher and deeper than ours; for our science seeks to explain what life is, aspires to understand it in order to teach others how to live, while they without science knew how to live; and that I understood, but I could not understand their knowledge. They showed me their trees, and I could not understand the intense love with which they looked at them; it was as though they were talking with creatures like themselves.

And perhaps I shall not be mistaken if I say that they conversed with them. Yes, they had found their language, and I am convinced that the trees understood them. They looked at all Nature like that—at the animals who lived in peace with them and did not attack them, but loved them, conquered by their love. They pointed to the stars and told me something about them which I could not understand, but I am convinced that they were somehow in touch with the stars, not only in thought, but by some living channel. Oh, these people did not persist in trying to make me understand them, they loved me without that, but I knew that they would never understand me, and so I hardly spoke to them about our earth.

I only kissed in their presence the earth on which they lived and mutely worshipped them themselves. And they saw that and let me worship them without being abashed at my adoration, for they themselves loved much. They were not unhappy on my account when at times I kissed their feet with tears, joyfully conscious of the love with which they would respond to mine. At times I asked myself with wonder how it was they were able never to offend a creature like me, and never once to arouse a feeling of jealousy or envy in me? Often I wondered how it could be that, boastful and untruthful as I was, I never talked to them of what I knew—of which, of course, they had no notion—that I was never tempted to do so by a desire to astonish or even to benefit them.

They were as gay and sportive as children. They wandered about their lovely woods and copses, they sang their lovely songs; their fare was light—the fruits of their trees, the honey from their woods, and the milk of the animals who loved them. The work they did for food and raiment was brief and not laborious. They loved and begot children, but I never noticed in them the impulse of that *cruel* sensuality which overcomes almost every man on this earth, all and each, and is the source of almost every sin of mankind on earth.

They rejoiced at the arrival of children as new beings to share their happiness. There was no quarrelling, no jealousy among them, and they did not even know what the words meant. Their children were the children of all, for they all made up one family. There was scarcely any illness among them, though there was death; but their old people died peacefully, as though falling asleep, giving blessings and smiles to those who surrounded them to take their last farewell with bright and loving smiles. I never saw grief or tears on those occasions, but only love, which reached the point of ecstasy, but a calm ecstasy, made perfect and contemplative.

One might think that they were still in contact with the departed after death, and that their earthly union was not cut short by death. They scarcely understood me when I questioned them about immortality, but evidently they were so convinced of it without reasoning that it was not for them a question at all. They had no temples, but they had a real living and uninterrupted sense of oneness with the whole of the universe; they had no creed, but they had a certain knowledge that when their earthly joy had reached the limits of earthly nature, then there would come for them, for the living and for the dead, a still greater fullness of contact with the whole of the universe. They looked forward to that moment with joy, but without haste, not pining for it, but seeming to have a foretaste of it in their hearts, of which they talked to one another.

In the evening before going to sleep they liked singing in musical and harmonious chorus. In those songs they expressed all the sensations that the parting day had given them, sang its glories and took leave of it. They sang the praises of nature, of the sea, of the woods. They liked making songs about one another, and praised each other like children; they were the simplest songs, but they sprang from their hearts and went to one's heart. And not only in their songs but in all their lives they seemed to do nothing but admire one another. It was like being in love with each other, but an all-embracing, universal feeling.

Some of their songs, solemn and rapturous, I scarcely understood at all. Though I understood the words I could never fathom their full significance. It remained, as it were, beyond the grasp of my mind, yet my heart unconsciously absorbed it more and more. I often told them that I had had a presentiment of it long before, that this joy and glory had come to me on our earth in the form of a yearning melancholy that at times approached insufferable sorrow; that I had had a foreknowledge of them all and of their glory in the dreams of my heart and the visions of my mind; that often on our earth I could not look at the setting sun without tears ... that in my hatred for the men of our earth there was always a yearning anguish: why could I not hate them without loving them? why could I not help forgiving them? and in my love for them there was a yearning grief: why could I not love them without hating them?

They listened to me, and I saw they could not conceive what I was saying, but I did not regret that I had spoken to them of it: I knew that they understood the intensity of my yearning anguish over those whom I had left. But when they looked at me with their sweet eyes full of love, when I felt that in their presence my heart, too, became as innocent and just as theirs, the feeling of the fullness of life took my breath away, and I worshipped them in silence.

Oh, every one laughs in my face now, and assures me that one cannot dream of such details as I am telling now, that I only dreamed or felt one sensation that arose in my heart in delirium and made up the details myself when I woke up. And when I told them that perhaps it really was so, my God, how they shouted with laughter in my face, and what mirth I caused! Oh, yes, of course I was overcome by the mere sensation of my dream, and that was all that was preserved in my cruelly wounded heart; but the actual forms and images of my dream, that is, the very ones I really saw at the very time of my dream, were filled with such harmony, were so lovely and enchanting and were so actual, that on awakening I was, of course, incapable of clothing them in our poor language, so that they were bound to become blurred in my mind; and so perhaps I really was forced afterwards to make up the details, and so of course to distort them in my passionate desire to convey some at least of them as quickly as I could.

But on the other hand, how can I help believing that it was all true? It was perhaps a thousand times brighter, happier and more joyful than I describe it. Granted that I dreamed it, yet it must have been real. You know, I will tell you a secret: perhaps it was not a dream at all! For then something happened so awful, something so horribly true, that it could not have been imagined in a dream. My heart may have originated the dream, but would my heart alone have been capable of originating the awful event which happened to me afterwards? How could I alone have invented it or imagined it in my dream? Could my petty heart and my fickle, trivial mind have risen to such a revelation of truth? Oh, judge for yourselves: hitherto I have concealed it, but now I will tell the truth. The fact is that I ... corrupted them all!

V

Yes, yes, it ended in my corrupting them all! How it could come to pass I do not know, but I remember it clearly. The dream embraced thousands of years and left in me only a sense of the whole. I only know that I was the cause of their sin and downfall. Like a vile trichina, like a germ of the plague infecting whole kingdoms, so I contaminated all this earth, so happy and sinless before my coming.

They learnt to lie, grew fond of lying, and discovered the charm of falsehood. Oh, at first perhaps it began innocently, with a jest, coquetry, with amorous play, perhaps indeed with a germ, but that germ of falsity made its way into their hearts and pleased them. Then sensuality was soon begotten, sensuality begot jealousy, jealousy—cruelty.... Oh, I don't know, I don't remember; but soon, very soon the first blood was shed.

They marvelled and were horrified, and began to be split up and divided. They formed into unions, but it was against one another. Reproaches, upbraidings followed. They came to know shame, and shame brought them to virtue. The conception of honour sprang up, and every union began waving its flags. They began torturing animals, and the animals withdrew from them into the forests and became hostile to them. They began to struggle for separation, for isolation, for individuality, for mine and thine. They began to talk in different languages. They became acquainted with sorrow and loved sorrow; they thirsted for suffering, and said that truth could only be attained through suffering. Then science appeared. As they became wicked they began talking of brotherhood and humanitarianism, and understood those ideas.

As they became criminal, they invented justice and drew up whole legal codes in order to observe it, and to ensure their being kept, set up a guillotine. They hardly remembered what they had lost, in fact refused to believe that they had ever been happy and innocent. They even laughed at the possibility of this happiness in the past, and called it a dream. They could not even imagine it in definite form and shape, but, strange and wonderful to relate, though they lost all faith in their past happiness and called it a legend, they so longed to be happy and innocent once more that they succumbed to this desire like children, made an idol of it, set up temples and worshipped their own idea, their own desire; though at the same time they fully believed that it was unattainable and could not be realised, yet they bowed down to it and adored it with tears! Nevertheless, if it could have happened that they had returned to the innocent and happy condition which they had lost, and if someone had shown it to them again and had asked them whether they wanted to go back to it, they would certainly have refused. They answered me:

"We may be deceitful, wicked and unjust, we *know* it and weep over it, we grieve over it; we torment and punish ourselves more perhaps than that merciful Judge Who will judge us and whose Name we know not. But we have science, and by means of it we shall find the truth and we shall arrive at it consciously. Knowledge is higher than feeling, the consciousness of life is higher than life. Science will give us wisdom, wisdom will reveal the laws, and the knowledge of the laws of happiness is higher than happiness."

That is what they said, and after saying such things every one began to love himself better than anyone else, and indeed they could not do otherwise. All became so jealous of the rights of their own personality that they did their very utmost to curtail and destroy them in others, and made that the chief thing in their lives.

Slavery followed, even voluntary slavery; the weak eagerly submitted to the strong, on condition that the latter aided them to subdue the still weaker. Then there were saints who came to these people, weeping, and talked to them of their pride, of their loss of harmony and due proportion, of their loss of shame. They were laughed at or pelted with stones.

Holy blood was shed on the threshold of the temples. Then there arose men who began to think how to bring all people together again, so that everybody, while still loving himself best of all, might not interfere with others, and all might live together in something like a harmonious society. Regular wars sprang up over this idea.

All the combatants at the same time firmly believed that science, wisdom and the instinct of self-preservation would force men at last to unite into a harmonious and rational society; and so, meanwhile, to hasten matters, "the wise" endeavoured to exterminate as rapidly as possible all who were "not wise" and did not understand their idea, that the latter might not hinder its triumph. But the instinct of self-preservation grew rapidly weaker; there arose men, haughty and sensual, who demanded all or nothing. In order to obtain everything they resorted to crime, and if they did not succeed—to suicide. There arose religions with a cult of non-existence and self-destruction for the sake of the everlasting peace of annihilation. At last these people grew weary of their meaningless toil, and signs of suffering came into their faces, and then they proclaimed that suffering was a beauty, for in suffering alone was there meaning.

They glorified suffering in their songs. I moved about among them, wringing my hands and weeping over them, but I loved them perhaps more than in old days when there was no suffering in their faces and when they were innocent and so lovely. I loved the earth they had polluted even more than when it had been a paradise, if only because sorrow had come to it.

Alas! I always loved sorrow and tribulation, but only for myself, for myself; but I wept over them, pitying them. I stretched out my hands to them in despair, blaming, cursing and despising myself. I told them that all this was my doing, mine alone; that it was I had brought them corruption, contamination and falsity. I besought them to crucify me, I taught them how to make a cross. I could not kill myself, I had not the strength, but I wanted to suffer at their hands. I yearned for suffering, I longed that my blood should be drained to the last drop in these agonies. But they only laughed at me, and began at last to look upon me as crazy. They justified me, they declared that they had only got what they wanted themselves, and that all that now was could not have been otherwise. At last they declared to me that I was becoming dangerous and that they should lock me up in a madhouse if I did not hold my tongue. Then such grief took possession of my soul that my heart was wrung, and I felt as though I were dying; and then ... then I awoke.

It was morning, that is, it was not yet daylight, but about six o'clock. I woke up in the same arm-chair; my candle had burnt out; everyone was asleep in the captain's room, and there was a stillness all round, rare in our flat. First of all I leapt up in great amazement: nothing like this had ever happened to me before, not even in the most trivial detail; I had never, for instance, fallen asleep like this in my arm-chair. While I was standing and coming to myself I suddenly caught sight of my revolver lying loaded, ready—but instantly I thrust it away! Oh, now, life, life! I lifted up my hands and called upon eternal truth, not with words but with tears; ecstasy, immeasurable ecstasy flooded my soul. Yes, life and spreading the good tidings! Oh, I at that moment resolved to spread the tidings, and resolved it, of course, for my whole life. I go to spread the tidings, I want to spread the tidings—of what? Of the truth, for I have seen it, have seen it with my own eyes, have seen it in all its glory.

And since then I have been preaching! Moreover I love all those who laugh at me more than any of the rest. Why that is so I do not know and cannot explain, but so be it. I am told that I am vague and confused, and if I am vague and confused now, what shall I be later on? It is true indeed: I am vague and confused, and perhaps as time goes on I shall be more so. And of course I shall make many blunders before I find out how to preach, that is, find out what words to say, what things to do, for it is a very difficult task. I see all that as clear as daylight, but, listen, who does not make mistakes?

And yet, you know, all are making for the same goal, all are striving in the same direction anyway, from the sage to the lowest robber, only by different roads. It is an old truth, but this is what is new: I cannot go far wrong. For I have seen the truth; I have seen and I know that people can be beautiful and happy without losing the power of living on earth. I will not and cannot believe that evil is the normal condition of mankind. And it is just this faith of mine that they laugh at. But how can I help believing it? I have seen the truth—it is not as though I had invented it with my mind, I have seen it, seen it, and *the living image* of it has filled my soul forever. I have seen it in such full perfection that I cannot believe that it is impossible for people to have it. And so how can I go wrong? I shall make some slips no doubt, and shall perhaps talk in second-hand language, but not for long: the living image of what I saw will always be with me and will always correct and guide me.

Oh, I am full of courage and freshness, and I will go on and on if it were for a thousand years! Do you know, at first I meant to conceal the fact that I corrupted them, but that was a mistake—that was my first mistake! But truth whispered to me that I was *lying*, and preserved me and corrected me. But how establish paradise—I don't know, because I do not know how to put it into words. After my dream I lost command of words. All the chief words, anyway, the most necessary ones. But never mind, I shall go and I shall keep talking, I won't leave off, for anyway I have seen it with my own eyes, though I cannot describe what I saw. But the scoffers do not understand that. It was a dream, they say, delirium, hallucination. Oh! As though that meant so much! And they are so proud! A dream! What is a dream? And is not our life a dream? I will say more.

Suppose that this paradise will never come to pass (that I understand), yet I shall go on preaching it. And yet how simple it is: in one day, *in one hour* everything could be arranged at once! The chief thing is to love others like yourself, that's the great thing, and that's everything; nothing else is wanted—you will find out at once how to arrange it all. And yet it's an old truth which has been told and retold a billion times—but it has not formed part of our lives! The consciousness of life is higher than life, the knowledge of the laws of happiness is higher than happiness—that is what one must contend against. And I shall. If only everyone wants it, it can all be arranged at once.

And I tracked out that little girl ... and I shall go on and on!

THE END

Discussion Question

Discuss the writing style of Fyodor Dostoyevsky. Do you believe he writes to provide entertainment or is there a deeper purposes to what he has to say?

Critical Thinking Exercise

Using crime behaviors, personality characteristics, criminological theories, and behavioral analysis of violent crime, identify in outline form how, if at all, these factors are represented in the short story, *The Dream of a Ridiculous Man*.

Made in the USA
Middletown, DE
07 September 2020

18863528R00121